FORFEITING
ALL SANITY

FORFEITING
ALL SANITY

A Mother's Story of Raising a Child with *Fetal Alcohol Syndrome*

Jennifer Poss Taylor

TATE PUBLISHING & *Enterprises*

Published by Tate Publishing & Enterprises, LLC
127 E. Trade Center Terrace | Mustang, Oklahoma 73064 USA
1.888.361.9473 | www.tatepublishing.com

Tate Publishing is committed to excellence in the publishing industry. The company reflects the philosophy established by the founders, based on Psalm 68:11,
"The Lord gave the word and great was the company of those who published it."

Book design copyright © 2010 by Tate Publishing, LLC. All rights reserved.
Cover design by Kandi Evans
Interior design by Kellie Southerland

Published in the United States of America

ISBN: 978-1-61566-812-0
1. Family & Relationships / Children With Special Needs
2. Family & Relationships / Parenting / General
10.01.14

For all who are led by the Spirit of God are children of God.

Romans 8:14

My beautiful blond, blue-eyed angel

To my sweet Ashley, there was a time I whispered in your ear every night, "I thank God for you." As you have grown into a young woman, I still thank God for you every day. I know we are in his almighty plan, and we have a mission together to teach others to "take care of babies while they are still in tummies." I also thank God that he lives in your heart and you know him. I thank you, Ashley, for forgiving me of my mistakes as I learn more about you each day. I have prayed for you specifically for as long as I can remember, and I will continue to pray for you as long as I live. Always remember that miracles happen to those who believe, and I know you, my angel, are a believer!

Mommy

ACKNOWLEDGMENTS

Ashley did not choose the right to give up her sanity. Instead, she unwillingly forfeited that right because her birthmother consumed alcohol while she was pregnant with Ashley. David, my husband, and I, however, willingly forfeited our right to maintain all sanity when we took on the challenge of adopting a child with developmental delays. We vowed to raise her to the best of our ability with Christ leading us every step of the way. We could not make it without the strength that God has given us.

I want to especially thank my dear friend, Kristin. You have been my sounding board each and every day of my life for the last ten years. Your words of wisdom, advice, support, and friendship mean more to me than anything you could ever imagine.

Thank you to sweet Faith, Ashley's best friend. Thank you for loving Ashley unconditionally. You are a true Godsend.

Dr. Nabulsi, just knowing you are only a phone call or e-mail away at any given moment gives us the confidence we need to offer Ashley every opportunity available to her.

I can't imagine going through any part of parenting

without you, David. You are a wonderful, patient husband and father. I thank God for you each day as we continue to cherish raising our family together.

Daddy, I am so blessed by your unconditional love and acceptance. I pray that I can pass those same qualities down to my children.

I also want to thank you, Mommy, for never giving up on me. I have learned to appreciate and respect you so much. Thank you for constantly correcting my grammar. I could not have picked a better person to walk me through the process of writing my very first book.

Danie, thank you so much for helping me proof this book during the final editing phase. I am so grateful you were more than willing to drop everything at the last minute. I know you have a busy life raising four beautiful girls. God has blessed me with a wonderful friend!

Finally, I want to thank everyone at Tate Publishing for offering me, an unknown author, the rare opportunity to publish this book. So many of your employees have offered prayers to help get the word out about fetal alcohol syndrome, which of course, is the goal of the book.

TABLE OF CONTENTS

FOREWORD

As a pastor I see family after family who encounter a wide variety of trials and challenges. While there are many families who succumb to the pressures of life, I have seen many more who put their trust in God, endure, and become a powerful testimony of hope for all to see.

Jennifer Poss Taylor and her precious husband and children are one of those families whom God is using to be a powerful voice of truth and an authentic model of patience and love. *Forfeiting All Sanity: A Mother's Story of Raising a Child with Fetal Alcohol Syndrome* is both informational and inspirational. It is a book that tackles a subject where, frankly, many people are uninformed or misinformed.

Several years ago, my wife Stephanie was finishing up her physical therapy degree and chose to write a paper on an issue I had never heard of before, called fetal alcohol syndrome. I remember very well her passion to warn moms of this serious issue. Now, all these years later, I am so grateful for the contribution Jennifer has made through the writing of this book.

Her passion for informing our generation about FAS

is combined with a real-life testimony of love, faithfulness, disappointment, heartache, and hope. I have seen time and again how God will take an individual or family who has encountered so many challenges and use them to make an incredible difference in the lives of other people. I am confident that God is raising Jennifer Taylor up to be a clear voice for a critical issue and an example for others to learn from and be inspired by.

It is obvious throughout the pages of *Forfeiting All Sanity* that Jennifer and her family have put their trust in Jesus Christ. He is their strength, their guide, and their passion. It is my prayer that as you read this book, you will come to know the power of Jesus Christ as well, because He will not only change your life, but He will help you face whatever challenge you are encountering today. He restores, rebuilds, and renews.

Jennifer Taylor and her family know this to be true. And I am glad that she is sharing her story with you today.

Blessings,
Brad Jurkovich
Senior Pastor, Victory Life Baptist Church
Lubbock, Texas

INTRODUCTION

He is the Rock, his work is perfect, Everything he
does is just and fair. He is a faithful God who does
no wrong; How just and upright he is!

Deuteronomy 32:4

When Ashley was first diagnosed with fetal alcohol syndrome (FAS), due to damage to the brain during pregnancy, I went to the store to purchase every book I could get my hands on. I had been formally educated in college and in my career on children with special needs, but when it was my own child, everything became a blur. As it turned out, there were very few books that pertained to Ashley. I did purchase everything I could find. I went straight home and began reading.

The books that I found were very discouraging, very dark, very boring, and very old. I was determined at that time to write a book that would be just the opposite. I wanted to write about all the rewarding attributes a child like Ashley possesses and how wonderful it can be to raise her with God on my side. After all, for fourteen years I prayed that I would one day have a child. How could I not enjoy every minute of raising Ashley, knowing that she is the answer to that specific prayer?

Now, four years after Ashley's diagnosis, I finally realize why some of the books I read during that initial time of trying to comprehend her terrible brain abnormality were so difficult for me to read. Those books focused on the negative behaviors only and not the blessing that God created. They failed to discuss why the children demonstrated certain behaviors, and they also failed to offer positive ways to handle those behaviors. I am thankful for the gift of humor and patience. Those gifts enable me to accept whatever challenge Ashley unintentionally throws my way. The gift of patience has allowed me to try various techniques or strategies on Ashley that may help her to function more appropriately.

HELLO, ASHLEY

Finally, he designated the amount of refined gold for the altar of incense and for the gold cherubim, whose wings were stretched out over the Ark of the Lord's covenant. "Every part of this plan," David told Solomon, "was given to me in writing from the hand of the Lord." Then David continued, "Be strong and courageous, and do the work. Don't be afraid or discouraged by the size of the task, for the Lord God, my God, is with you. He will not fail you or forsake you. He will see to it that all the work related to the Temple of the Lord is finished correctly."

1 Chronicles 28:18–20

I can remember talking about baby names with my friends when I was in early elementary school. I had always known that one day I would be a mommy. But at the age of sixteen, the doctors tried to challenge my dreams. I had to see a team of specialists due to some hormonal and developmental abnormalities. I was told I was in the early stages of menopause and that I would never have children. The doctor said it was medically impossible, giving me less than a one percent chance of parenthood.

When he asked if I understood, I answered with strength and confidence, "Yes, I will have a child. Miracles happen to those who believe."

That night, I got down on my hands and knees and prayed for a blond, blue-eyed girl that looked just like me. I prayed every night for the next fourteen years. I prayed faithfully, never missing a night, never saying it differently, and never doubting that one day my prayer would be answered.

Then one night, fourteen years later, the phone rang. That was when my prayer was answered in God's perfect timing. A little blond, blue-eyed angel was heading my way.

One night, my husband, David, and I had just turned on a movie. The phone rang, and we hesitated to answer it because we did not want to be disturbed, but something took over both our souls at that point. An irresistible desire to simply answer the phone altered our lives. It was a friend of ours, who knew of our dream for a child. She called to tell us about a little girl who was up for adoption.

The little girl was in custody of the state but she was staying with her aunt and needed to be placed in a permanent home. She had blond hair and blue eyes, and according to our friend, she looked just like me. Our friend gave us the aunt's number and said if we were interested, the aunt would like to talk to us.

I hung up the phone with a pounding heart, and my eyes filled up with enormously happy tears. I told David this was our miracle from God. I remember seeing him sitting on the edge of the sofa. His hands were clasped together resting against his face with his right pointer covering his quivering lip. He too had tears in his eyes. We both were sure it was the same little girl that another friend had seen several months before when he dropped his own daughter off at dance. The fact that she was not already snatched up for adoption would just confirm to us that she was indeed our miracle. We called the aunt within minutes after we hung up the phone, but we had to leave a message.

Needless to say, we never finished that movie. Instead, we sat face to face discussing our dreams of having a child, this child. I went to bed that night eager to continue my nightly prayer that had become a routine, "Please God, I pray for a blond, blue-eyed girl that looks just like me."

We called again the next day and again the day after that. The aunt finally called us back. It took a few days for her to return our call because it was not an easy decision for her to allow Ashley to be adopted. She struggled with the choice of wanting to raise Ashley herself. She was determined to make the best choice for Ashley, and finding the perfect family was the most important thing to her. It turned out her niece was the same baby who had been at the dance studio. They had been to the dance studio to meet the instructor who was also interested in adopting her. She was only there that one day. The possibility for the dance teacher to adopt her was not in God's plan. God's plan did, however, include us. Little did we know, his plan had been in progress since I was in college.

I graduated from Texas Tech University with a Bachelor of Science in Human Development and Family Studies.

I chose this degree for very personal reasons. My high school years were tough. I lived with my father who had a drinking problem. My mother and I had grown very far apart. It was almost like therapy for me to go to class each day. I was determined to learn as much as I could about family dynamics so I could not only help myself but help other people in difficult situations as well.

Once I graduated, I moved to Fort Worth, Texas, to complete an internship as a child life specialist, normalizing the environment for children in the hospital. I also educated the children and the parents on specific illnesses and medical procedures, as well as created different coping mechanisms for them to handle their challenges. I had a couple of jobs after my internship, including a position specifically working with children birth to age three who had special needs. I served as a parent trainer and educator where I would go into the homes weekly to educate the parents and work with the children one-on-one.

During this time, I was also working on my masters degree in educational diagnostics. Although I was very passionate about my job, I had to change careers and give up my plans of earning a masters degree due to financial reasons. It is a shame that most careers that actually make a difference in people's lives do not pay very much. I ended up getting into sales in order to pay my bills. I started out in insurance sales then moved to advertising.

My job as a yellow page sales representative had many perks. I loved the money, the freedom, and better yet, I fell in love with my boss! David and I married less than a year after I started working for him. David and I had actually crossed paths several times during college.

Although we never met in college, we each have pictures of us at the same parties with each other's friends.

God was definitely getting his plan in place. He led me in the direction of getting all the formal education and professional experience to raise typical children as well as children with special needs, and then he led me straight into the path of the man that would soon become the father to my children! God is awesome, and I continuously stand in wonderment by him.

Awesome Daddy

The aunt and I talked several times before we set a time to meet. Driving up to the home where Ashley was living was one of the most exciting days of my life. We walked up to the door to ring the doorbell, and we saw this little angel in a white, ruffled dress perched on her beautiful aunt's hip. The aunt was making dinner for her family, and Ashley seemed to be watching her every move from the best seat in the house.

Ashley was around nineteen months old. She was incredibly small. She wore glasses which magnified her big, blue eyes that seemed to overpower the rest of her pale face. She had only been walking a few weeks.

As we sat on the couch talking to the aunt, I tried everything I could to quietly get Ashley's attention. I would smile at her, and she would just turn her head ever so slightly so she could still see me out of the corner of her eye. Then, as if I had been to that house a million times, I decided I would slide off the edge of the couch and make myself comfortable on the carpet. Within minutes, *my* baby was sitting in my lap playing games with me while David and I discussed intimate details about the baby's past, the aunt's hopes, and our dreams with the biological family.

The aunt told us the little girl's name was Ashley Rae Ann. She was her brother's daughter. The aunt did not even know Ashley existed until Christmas Eve 2000 when she received a heart-wrenching call. Child Protective Services picked Ashley up at a battered woman's homeless shelter the day before Christmas, just a few days before her first birthday. She was severely malnourished, neglected, and very ill.

I was told that when Ashley was picked up, she was sleeping in a stroller on top of soiled diapers. She had a curdled bottle of diluted milk clutched in her delicate hands that she was protecting as if it were her last meal. If they had not come when they did, it very well could have been her last day.

Ashley's aunt and grandparents spent nine months after they took her into their home nursing Ashley back to health. They spent a fortune on doctor visits and special formula that Ashley's sensitive tummy could handle. They had hoped the formula would also help to build up her immune system as well as help her growth. She still weighed only thirteen pounds after nine months of healthy nutrition. She wore clothes and shoes for a nine-month-old baby when we met her at nineteen months. She was extremely petite, and her features were very much distorted.

The visit went very well until it was time to leave. I felt like I was abandoning my child when I walked out the door and stepped up into my SUV, which would perfectly fit a car seat. I handed the family a letter that I wrote to them regarding our promises in regard to raising Ashley. Although we scheduled our next visit before we left, I could hardly leave her. I knew God had created her for me, and how could I possibly walk away?

Since Ashley was custody of the state, we had to handle things a little differently. The next visit was scheduled at our home. This time she was going to stay the day with us. The uncle dropped her off early one morning about a week later. We got to put her down for a nap, feed her, and, of course, take her shopping.

Again, it was great until she had to leave. The uncle picked her up late that afternoon, and I cried like I was the same age as Ashley. I knew I would see her again in a couple of days, but they could not come fast enough. For the next six weeks, while working through many hoops to start the adoption process, Ashley came to visit us every weekend. On Thanksgiving, she came to stay with us and never had to leave again.

Our first Christmas with Ashley

I remember asking Child Protective Services, once Ashley started living with us, if Ashley could have Down's syndrome or fetal alcohol syndrome. Down's syndrome is a genetic disorder, and fetal alcohol syndrome, often referred to as FAS, is a preventable brain abnormality caused by the consumption of alcohol by a pregnant woman. The alcohol prevents the brain from developing properly while the baby is in the womb. I was concerned because of her distorted features, a wide spread between her eyes, and a flatter than normal upper lip—all of which are indicators of FAS. But she also had some characteristics very much like a child with Down's syndrome. Along with a few anomalies or irregular facial features, I noticed some additional developmental delays that were starting to surface, such as delayed walking, talking, and self-help skills. I knew a little about both of these abnormalities because of my background in working with children with special needs. I knew that if she did have a genetic disorder or a brain abnormality that early intervention would be very beneficial.

After questioning Child Protective Services about Ashley's possible abnormalities, the department sent Ashley to a geneticist to test for various genetic disorders, including Down's syndrome after I specifically requested it. The geneticist made the determination after blood work and a few measurements that Ashley did not have a genetic disorder. The department also provided an in-depth investigation with the mother to determine FAS. They made a quick phone call, asked the mother if she drank during pregnancy, and, of course, the mother said no. That was that. I was told that Ashley could not possibly have FAS according to their investigation. The physicians involved at the time prepared us for the possibility that Ashley would indeed struggle with various developmental delays that would become more noticeable the older she got due to the neglect and malnourishment she experienced. She might even struggle with school due to undisclosed genetic factors. We were aware that Ashley would have medical needs regarding her vision, and eye surgery had already been discussed. We felt confident we could handle anything that the future might bring. I was well educated in this area and had an abundance of professional experience with other families dealing with these very circumstances.

At one point during the adoption process, we were actually supervising the court-appointed weekly visits in our own home. Once the facts were out in the open as far as Ashley having special needs, the birthmother knew without a doubt that she could not provide for Ashley with those needs. She could not provide for Ashley even without any special circumstances.

The birthmother was pregnant again from another man. She was very responsive as far as seeing Ashley for her weekly visits, and it was evident that she truly loved Ashley. It was also evident that the father of her unborn child was very aware of the possibility of the state taking their baby if the case was still open.

The birthmother had failed to give Ashley, while in her "care," the medical attention she needed—not to mention the proper nutrition. The birthmother easily qualified for governmental assistance. I don't know if she was too lazy to get the assistance or too uneducated to know about the assistance she could have received. If the latter is the case, then the system failed Ashley. Someone somewhere, probably the birthmother's medical provider, should have spent time educating the mother on how to receive help and should have made sure someone was assigned to assist her in following through with her responsibilities as an expectant parent.

In December of that same year, after only fostering Ashley in our home for two short months, the birthmother relinquished her own rights. The judge pounded her desk with the gavel, announcing that "the Taylor's could officially begin the adoption process."

The adoption went so smoothly that even the caseworker made the comment that she had never handled a case that went through like ours did. Child Protective Service's main goal is to reunite the children with the family, if at all possible, after providing educational counseling and parental training. The birthfather's rights were already relinquished because of a poor choice he had made. He evidently spanked Ashley or abused her physically, which was proven in the court system. He lost his rights to ever be around her again.

Thankfully, his parents were angels that were also placed on this earth to protect Ashley, and he knew that when his father spoke, he needed to listen. The birthfather knew better than to fight the system because if he did, he would have to face his own father. We met the birthfather one time the very first Christmas we celebrated with Ashley, when Ashley's aunt invited us to her house to be with the whole family.

After celebrating Ashley's second birthday in January, we became Ashley Wynn Taylor's legal Mommy and Daddy in May 2002! We did not think it was fair to her by the age of two to change her first name; however, we did change her middle name to Wynn, after my father.

Adoption day picture with our attorney and the judge

Flower petals from our baby shower

WELCOME TO PARENTHOOD

Now I am coming to you for the third time, and I will not be a burden to you. I don't want what you have; I want you. And anyway, little children don't pay for their parents' food. It's the other way around; parents supply food for their children. I will gladly spend myself and all I have for your spiritual good, even though it seems that the more I love you, the less you love me.

2 Corinthians 12:14–15

Woo hoo! God answers prayer. I had a car seat in my car, a baby crib in my home, and I owned a baby stroller. My home was filled with the pitter-patter of little feet and lots of giggles. This was the life I had always dreamed of.

I reminded myself daily of that conversation in the doctor's office when I was sixteen years old. "Yes, I will have a child!" I wanted to reenact that scene in *Pretty Woman* where Julia Roberts walked into the store that declined her service and prance into the doctor's office with my beautiful baby and say, "See, I told you so. Big, big, mistake."

Oh so cute!

We enjoyed each and every minute of our new adventure. I loved dressing Ashley up and sporting her around town. She was even asked to be a model for one of the local baby stores. At the time, we thought her tiny body was adorable, and it was. We did not realize how much smaller she was than other two-year-olds. In a way, for me, it was like getting to enjoy a child that was much younger than two—a gift I thought I would never experience.

Ashley's eyes were so much larger than the rest of her features. I just assumed her eyes gave the illusion they were crossing. Her feet were still abnormally small at the time. I bought tons of sassy, little shoes to go with every outfit. The thought never crossed my mind that it was difficult for her to walk in them. Come to think of it, she didn't have to walk much. She was always on my hip. It did not take me long to notice that looking cute was far more important to me than it was to her.

All dressed up

Bath time quickly became a favorite time for the whole family. I laugh at the picture of the first time the Taylor family came to our home for Thanksgiving, which was the same time Ashley first came to live with us. During bath time, all seventeen of us, including our dog, Andy, piled into our bathroom to watch Ashley as she frolicked around in our large, oversized soaking tub, smiling from ear to ear due to all of the overabundance of love and attention she was now receiving.

Cleanliness became alarmingly concerning. It was far

more fun for me to bathe Ashley and keep her clean than it was for her to keep herself clean. It was different from most toddlers who stayed dirty like Pigpen on Charlie Brown. Not only did Ashley not care if she was dirty or had food strung from one side of her face to the other, she was completely unaware of the sticky or gooey substance that hid her beauty.

When I dreamed of baby names when I was in grade school, I also dreamed of taking my children to activities just like those I participated in. I enrolled Ashley in ballet when she was two, knowing she would love it. However, it was a nightmare because she was so shy and easily frightened. In my mind, I thought it would bring out the extrovert that I knew had to be in my child. I tend to forget at times that we do not actually share the same genes.

On days that parents watched, she literally hid in a corner crying. At the time, I was embarrassed. I wondered what people thought of my child. She was the only one acting out like that, and I knew it was not going unnoticed.

Swimming lessons were a different story. Ashley has loved the water from the moment her "bear cub" feet, as her Daddy calls them, touched the water for the very first time. At one point, she told everyone she was going to be a diver one day. The water has always given her a sense of freedom that she simply cannot get anywhere else. I am certain that is why she loved to play in our huge tub for hours. I noticed quickly, however, that she was the only one at swimming lessons who would impatiently wait her turn, licking all the water off her toes, up her legs, and down her arms. I tapped on the viewing window numerous times, shaking my finger at her and reminding her to quit licking herself like a cat lying in front of a warm, sunny window.

Ashley attended a mom's day out program at one of the local churches the following fall. The very first day of school, I got a call which started off with, "Ashley is okay, but …" It turned out that she was fighting with a little boy over a toy. They both ran for it at the same time, and the top of his head hit her eye socket. Yes, the first day of school was also her first shiner and the first of many calls from school starting out with, "Ashley is okay, but…"

First day of Mom's Day Out

We were so grateful for Ashley after the adoption was final and the realization that my prayer for a child had finally been answered. Once I got into the routine of being a stay at home mommy and running Ashley to all of her activities, we decided to pray for more children. We made another choice to stay active with the foster parents association.

We felt greedy asking God for another child when we

were so blessed with Ashley, but we desperately wanted to help other children in Ashley's situation as much as we possibly could, and we loved parenthood. We fostered several children early on, knowing that it was just for a short time, as well as two other children that at the time were very possibly going to be adoptable. It was an unexplainable feeling when the two children that were possibly adoptable arrived at our house just a few days before our second Christmas with Ashley. We were partly excited about the fact that our family might increase but a little hesitant to celebrate because of the issues they each had. Their specific case was so bad it was actually used as part of the training for the state employees. The girl was a little over a year older than Ashley, and the boy was about a year younger.

Toys, toys, toys

Beep, beep, watch out Mommy!

By Valentine's Day 2003, it was just the three of us again. We no longer had the two foster children. Just one month later, we were planning a trip to Lubbock, Texas, for Ashley to have eye surgery. One eye completely turned in, and shut itself off from viewing her happy little world. By now it was apparent that her eye truly crossed and it was not just an illusion. I have to admit, I have always thought Ashley looked so cute in her little glasses. She has actually worn them since she was only thirteen months old.

The first time we met her, she had almost doll-sized, gold-rimmed glasses with pink rubber ear loops. The glasses magnified her huge, beautiful blue eyes. I had her first three pairs of glasses framed. I can't even count how many we have purchased since that first tiny pair. We decided that if she was going to have to wear them, then we might as well make them a fashion accessory. Again, having the fancy glasses was probably more for me than for her, but it has helped to teach her colors. At one point, she had about six pairs in various stylish shades of colors.

Struggling to focus in the sun

In the middle of all the planning for the surgery, I suddenly got this overwhelming sense of nesting. I told David that for some reason I felt like God was going to grant us another one of our prayers. I felt like we were about to be blessed with a little boy to foster and adopt. I frantically began setting up our guest room as a nursery. I put Ashley's crib back together. She only slept in it a short while before she started screaming just at the thought of having to get in it. I also brought the glider upstairs and strategically placed a nightlight and a CD player beside it. I had never actually had an infant in my home, but I knew without a doubt that was going to change.

Ashley's surgery was at the end of March in 2003, and it was very successful. She handled it like a trooper, and now her huge blue eyes were more beautiful than ever as they both stared directly at me simultaneously. We returned home to take the next couple of days somewhat easy.

Ashley and I were lying on the couch the next day watching *The Wiggles* when the phone rang. It was Child Protective Services. There was a newborn baby boy in the neonatal intensive care unit that needed a foster home to go to once he was well enough to leave the hospital. Although he was legally given another name, we called him Grant from the moment we met him because we felt like God was granting us our prayer for another child.

Only six weeks after we brought Grant home, we received another call. This time, it was about a teenage mom who heard about us from a friend. The mother lived in another town, but a lady at her school was a friend of a friend of ours. They told her how we could not medically have children and how we adopted Ashley, fostered children, and we were fostering Grant with hopes to adopt him.

The mother was pregnant with a baby girl due in October. We were honored that she thought of us. But would it be crazy to have two babies only seven months apart? We said thank you, but we just couldn't handle another baby at the time. God had other plans because we heard from the family again just a few months later. We agreed to meet the family, and it became apparent that God led us to one another. Needless to say, this one was my "surprise pregnancy" because only six months after bringing home a brother to Ashley, she was blessed with a baby sister as well.

In the meantime, we had moved to a much-needed bigger house. Ashley was very proud to be the big sister. We were definitely proud parents now with not only one, but three car seats, two cribs, and a triple stroller. (Not to mention the Barbie tent that seemed to be a permanent fixture in our master bedroom.) When Grant arrived, he slept in a port-a-crib in our room. Ashley decided to pull her Barbie tent in our room and placed it at the foot of our bed. She slept in it many months. Once we started tripping over her feet in the middle of the night as they stuck out the end of the tent, we decided it was time for her to go back to her big girl bed and Grant had to go to his room. After all, we had a newborn baby girl sharing the room with us. Rapidly, parenthood permanently entered our lives with a bang, bang, bang!

Moments after Ashley's eye surgery

The proud big sister

Ashley's Barbie tent at the foot of our bed

Three Christmas miracles

DIAGNOSIS

So take a new grip with your tired hands and stand
firm on your shaky legs. Mark out a straight path for
your feet. Then those who follow you, though they
are weak and lame, will not stumble and fall but will
become strong.

Hebrews 12:12–13

The older Ashley got, the more apparent her differences
became. I was completely aware of the fact that she would
have some developmental delays because of the experiences
she succumbed to her first few years of life, and I was prepared to work diligently with her on each of her delays. I was
not prepared, however, to handle the behavioral challenges
that each day presented that were so uncommon with other
children her age. We were told by other developmental
specialists that Ashley was about two years behind socially,
but even then, some of her actions were unique. We found
ourselves not only praying but begging God for answers on
how to handle some of Ashley's eccentricities.

By five, Ashley's differences started affecting the other kids in her classroom. She had started kindergarten at a private Christian school by this point where she had attended preschool for the two previous years. Her teacher began voicing her concerns. Ashley constantly had her hands on things she shouldn't, as well as all over her friends. She destroyed everything she touched, which at this point we assumed was still just an accident due to her lack of coordination and inability to handle certain objects because of fine motor delays.

Ashley's teacher pointed out several new, very alarming concerns. Ashley was literally eating a pencil a day. She would gnaw on it until it was a nub. She would sit on her desk and spin in circles, and she had a very difficult time relating socially to the other kids her age. She would get lost in the halls and tended to fall a lot. Ashley was also starting to show huge signs of frustration at home and at school. She became very defiant and seemed to be angry most of the time.

First day of kindergarten

We tried to get help from our pediatrician, who just kept telling me everything was normal. I took things into my own hands and enrolled her into speech therapy, physical therapy, and occupational therapy. We were given many possible diagnoses from the therapists, including joint laxity, ocular albinism, and sensory integration disorder. You name it! We were given idea after idea on how to help her cope with her destructiveness and compulsive behaviors.

Mouthing everything and having to touch everything seemed to be the main culprit at the time. Considering I had a background teaching children to cope with various behaviors and anxieties, you would think these ideas would have come naturally to me, but they did not. Everything I tried did not work, and soon the therapists realized that everything they were taught to try did not work with Ashley either.

One therapist suggested making Ashley a necklace out of fish tank tubing. The hope was that when she got nervous or over stimulated and needed to mouth something or touch something, she could use her necklace. Fish tank tubing is used often because of its durability. Ashley, on the other hand, was able to destroy the tubing within the first day, similar to the way a dog would destroy a bone.

At the same time we began getting concerned with Ashley, we started noticing some concerning things about our son, Grant, who is three years younger than Ashley. His habits, or talents should we say, were totally different than Ashley's, but we knew for sure they were not ordinary traits for someone his age either. At one point, a therapist talked to me about a seminar that was in town on sensory integration disorder. After hearing what was said, I was convinced we needed answers for not only Ashley, but Grant as well.

We were confident that Grant had a form of autism, but our pediatrician at the time said he was just fine as he smiled a cocky grin and advised me to quit reading books and enjoy being a mommy! As my "mommy horns" grew several inches high, I seriously considered putting my head down and trying one of those football player moves, plowing him flat to the ground. Wishing my horns were not imaginary but actually sharp enough to puncture, I calmly walked out of his office with my book on Asperger's syndrome and three kids in tow.

Six months later, I went back in that doctor's office demanding he make a referral for Grant to see an autism specialist in Lubbock, Texas. With a professional smirk, he finally said he would make the referral if I was staying awake at night worrying about it but that he highly doubted the doctor would diagnose Grant with anything before he was three, and he was positive Grant did not have autism. Once he finished his first of many more condescending remarks, I mentioned my concerns with Ashley. He then said, "What? Do you want me to refer her too?" I said in a very matter-of-fact way, "Yes, I do." I grabbed the much-needed referrals for not only insurance purposes, but also in an attempt to prove my sanity, and marched out of that office knowing that I would never step foot in there again.

Finally, some friends in our Sunday school class heard of our anguish over trying to find answers as to why Ashley was having so many struggles, and they gave us the name of their pediatrician, Dr. Sari Nabulsi. I called his office that same day to make an appointment. We were actually able to get in to see him before the behavior specialist that our previous pediatrician had unwillingly referred us to.

Ashley's fifth birthday

Dr. Nabulsi took the time to talk to me directly the very first time I called. We were hoping to at least get some solid answers on Grant, our son, so we could begin early intervention. We knew it was not normal for Grant to be reading at sixteen months old and yet not be able to call us by name or ask for something he desperately wanted or needed.

We briefly asked Dr. Nabulsi about Ashley. Dr. Nabulsi asked us to gather all medical records, any records we had on the biological history including state records, and to write down all of our concerns. He asked us to drop all of that off by his office before the appointment so he could study them thoroughly before we met.

David and I considered the possibility that she was not ready for kindergarten. If that was the case, we would willingly pull her out to give her more time. We also seriously considered the fact that Ashley was just acting out due to all the changes in the last couple of years. After all, we had only had Ashley a little over a year when we brought Grant home from the hospital, and it was only seven months after that when we brought Brooke, our youngest daughter, home from the hospital. Although she was so proud to be a big sister, getting two siblings so quickly would send almost anyone into a tailspin.

Lots of laughter

Around the same time as I made the initial phone call to Dr. Nabulsi, I began to take some concerns into my own hands once again, and I researched therapies for children with tactile/sensory issues and speech issues. Unfortunately, the choices in our hometown were very limited. I found a wonderful facility a couple of hours away in Lubbock, called Pediatric Therapy, Inc. I called to set up evaluations for Ashley and Grant. At the initial meeting,

I learned of many other therapies they offered, including feeding therapy, which would benefit both kids.

Finally, the day arrived for our very first visit with Dr. Nabulsi. During the appointment he thoroughly investigated Ashley's eyes, ears, and hands for the very first time as if inspecting a newborn moments after birth. And then he began asking us questions like he had been watching us the last few years. He nailed everything. I'll never forget the next thing that came out of his mouth. He wanted to run some extensive testing. He felt certain Ashley had a brain abnormality. Those words hit us like a ton of bricks. *A brain abnormality? What? She is just a little behind in development and possibly experiencing a severe case of the "jealousies,"* we thought to ourselves.

The next few weeks were rough. I began researching as fast as my fingers could type on the Internet. I would type in key words like *delays, vision abnormalities, behavioral issues, muscle weaknesses, failure to thrive.* I searched for any keyword I could think of that was remotely related to far too many unanswered questions we had begged doctors to answer. I had convinced myself that Ashley had shaken baby syndrome, knowing the few, yet horrifying, details of what her first year on this earth entailed living with her birthmother. I realized it was highly probable that in a moment of drunkenness or an alcohol-related brawl by the birthmother, or the birthfather for that matter, Ashley could have been considered a nuisance to anyone in her world. I hated to think of what they could have done or did do to her during that time. I can't bear to think of what her life would be like today if Child Protective Services had not rescued her when they did.

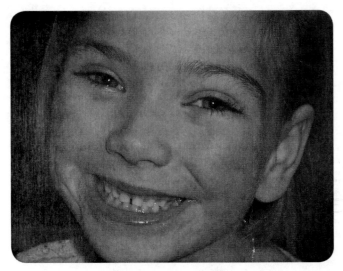

Close-up of Ashley's face, showing flat nose bridge and philtrum, and distance of eyes

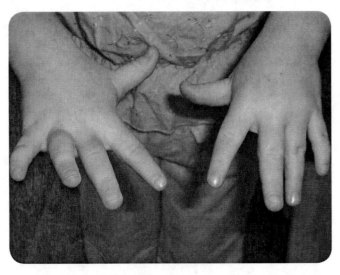

Close-up of Ashley's sweet hands with tiny pinkie fingers

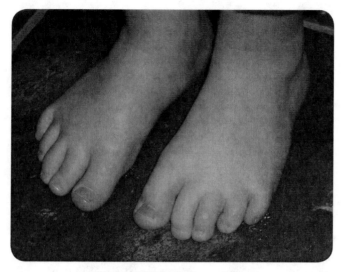

Close-up of Ashley's "bear cub" feet

We got the news from Dr. Nabulsi about two weeks after that first appointment. We had to wait for the results from the testing to get in. Dr. Nabulsi had sent us for an MRI, seizure testing, and bloodwork. I had just stepped out of the shower when the phone rang. I saw it was Dr. Nabulsi, so I grabbed the phone quickly.

I stood there holding a towel up against me, dripping wet and shaking with anticipation. I heard him say he wanted to call me as soon as he knew for sure. He said that yes, Grant had autism, which we were expecting, but he said it was a rare form that you only see once in a lifetime. Grant would be a struggle to keep challenged because he was incredibly intelligent. Then he proceeded to tell us that Ashley had fetal alcohol syndrome.

I began crying as I heard the diagnosis. I remembering hearing Dr. Nabulsi ask, "Are you okay? I am so sorry." The first thing I said was that we had asked about FAS when we first adopted Ashley. They assured us it wasn't that. I was mad at myself for not being more persistent in getting answers when Ashley was younger. I felt like I had wasted so much valuable time. I could have covered her with early intervention and every therapy available for her.

I could tell he was genuinely concerned and full of empathy as he delivered the news. He scheduled a time for us to come in and talk to him one-on-one and set up a treatment plan for both kids. To this day, he still puts his whole heart in everything he does with not only our family, but all of his patients. He is truly one of a kind.

When we went back in to the doctor, David just did not get it. He told Dr. Nabulsi that he was concerned for me. He said I acted as if I thought Ashley would never be able to live on her own. The doctor looked at David and said quietly, "That is very possible." I'll never forget the look on David's face and the weight I saw on his shoulders. He did not say anything else throughout the rest of the appointment. We got back in the car, and I told him to talk to me. I asked him, "What are you thinking?" He looked up at me with huge tears in his eyes and said, "It's not fair; it's just not fair." By this point, he cried in pain as he continued, saying, "She has been through so much already. Why should she have to go through this too?"

Now we both know why God chose Ashley and why he chose us. He knew what a powerful team we would be and how we would make it our mission to stop pregnant women from drinking. It is illegal to serve a minor alcohol. It is illegal to drink while driving. It should be illegal to drink while pregnant. A pregnant woman who chooses to drink alcohol at any time during her pregnancy is making the selfish decision to torture her innocent child. If the alcohol affects the child, the effects will last the entire lifetime of the child. The effects of alcohol on an unborn child are far more severe than any other drug and result in permanent damage to the child's brain, possible damage to the child's organs, and in some cases cause severe deformities in the child's appearance.

I know not all women know they are pregnant at first. In Ashley's case, as mad as I can get at her birthmother, I also realize she was not living in the best of circumstances nor does she function mentally according to her age. From what I have been told, she was almost three months pregnant before she knew. Although a part of me cannot fully comprehend that, I am very aware that in some cases that can happen. I also know that Ashley's birthmother loves Ashley very much and wanted the best for her; that is why she wanted us to adopt her. The birthmother herself experienced a less-than-desirable childhood which created a less-than-desirable adulthood. She made many poor decisions mostly because of men—including Ashley's birthfather, who indeed had issues with alcohol himself. I can say with complete confidence that she had no idea that she was hurting Ashley before birth. I believe it was up to her medical providers to educate her, and I believe they failed to do so.

I also know of another story where the mother was in her late forties to early fifties. She understandably thought she was going through the change of life. She and her friends who were also experiencing the change decided to celebrate this new adventure together on a trip to Mexico. They drank and relaxed and enjoyed life as they felt they should. They were not harming anyone. She returned to find out she was not going through the change of life; however, her life was in fact going to change. She was pregnant. Due to the celebration, her child was born with fetal alcohol syndrome. The mother in this particular situation can certainly not be blamed. She was not being careless or ruthless, much less criminal. However, her child will not be normal, and they will never experience normalcy again.

I can only imagine the guilt a mother must feel when she gets the news that her child will suffer because of something she intentionally did and it could have been 100 percent preventable. In most cases, the children that are actually diagnosed with fetal alcohol syndrome are children who have been adopted. I can't imagine going to the doctor's office and having to say, "I think I gave my child a brain abnormality because I just could not resist that glass of wine at the office party." There are many women who feel that just one glass of wine will not hurt their baby. That is simply not true. There is no amount of alcohol that is safe for the baby during pregnancy. It is true that some women can drink and the baby will not be affected at all, but it is also true that one drink can cause severe damage. It is just not worth the risk.

Any mother who drank during pregnancy and is facing difficulties with her child should strongly consider having an honest, open conversation with her physician about her concerns so the child can be assessed for FAS. If FAS is the diagnosis, then the proper treatment, therapy, and education would be in the best interest of the child. Many children are diagnosed with ADD or ADHD rather than FAS because the mother would not admit to drinking during pregnancy. These kids struggle socially and academically beyond the ADD/ADHD spectrum, and they need further treatment. Sometimes a behavior specialist can diagnose the child rather than a pediatrician.

A counselor or psychologist may not always be able to

diagnose the syndrome without running further medical exams. The child may be just fine, but he deserves proper medical attention. I highly suggest visiting www.nofas.org to view other clinical indicators for determining fetal alcohol syndrome.

According to the National Organization for Fetal Alcohol Syndrome, fetal alcohol syndrome is defined as a set of physical and mental birth defects that can result when a woman drinks alcohol during her pregnancy. When a pregnant woman drinks alcohol, such as beer, wine, or mixed drinks, so does her baby. Alcohol passes through the placenta right into the developing baby. The baby may suffer lifelong damage as a result.

Fetal alcohol syndrome is characterized by brain damage, facial deformities, and growth deficits. Heart, liver, and kidney defects also are common, as well as vision and hearing problems. Individuals with FAS have difficulties with learning, attention, memory, and problem solving.

Fetal Alcohol Spectrum Disorders (FASD) is an umbrella term describing the range of effects that can occur in an individual whose mother drank alcohol during pregnancy. These effects may include physical, mental, behavioral, and/or learning disabilities with possible lifelong implications. The term FASD is not intended for use as a clinical diagnosis.

FASD covers other terms such as:

- Fetal alcohol syndrome (FAS)–the only diagnosis given by doctors.

- Alcohol-related neurodevelopment disorder (ARND)–reserved for individuals with functional or cognitive impairments linked to prenatal alcohol exposure, including decreased head size at birth, structural brain abnormalities, and a pattern of behavioral and mental abnormalities.

- Alcohol-related birth defects (ARBD)– describes the physical defects linked to prenatal alcohol exposure, including heart, skeletal, kidney, ear, and eye malformations.

- Fetal alcohol effects (FAE)–a term that has been popularly used to describe alcohol-exposed individuals whose condition does not meet the full criteria for an FAS diagnosis.

All of the above information was provided by www. nofas.org. This Web site has a wealth of information and resources to help families, educators, and physicians for all issues related to fetal alcohol syndrome.

My photogenic child always ready for the camera

THE REALITY

Physical exercise has some value, but spiritual exercise is much more important, for it promises a reward in both this life and the next. This is true, and everyone should accept it. We work hard and suffer much in order that people will believe the truth, for our hope is in the living God, who is the Savior of all people, and particularly of those who believe.

1 Timothy 4: 8–10

I remember five days within the next five months after the diagnosis that I did not cry. I replayed all the conversations with Dr. Nabulsi in my head throughout the day. David changed jobs and poured himself into his work. I felt like he was not there for me, and maybe I was mad at him that he was able to focus on something other than the kids when that was all I could think about. It was horrible. I suffered from so much guilt. I knew what happened to Ashley was not my fault. My guilt, however, stemmed from not knowing, not being more aggressive in trying to help her. I should have disciplined differently.

I should have understood her more. I felt like a horrible mother. Every single problem we ever had replayed in my head over and over, and I was mortified at how I had been raising her. I felt as if all my dreams had been shattered. I didn't think it was fair to her, but I also didn't think it was fair to me, David, Grant, or Brooke.

Reality set in with Grant's diagnosis too. Yes, we were determined to get his diagnosis so that we could provide help for him, but we never thought about what autism really means; how it would affect our family; his social life; and again, how it would affect Brooke to have not one, but two siblings with special needs. I questioned whether or not I was worthy enough to be blessed by Ashley. I then went from wondering if someone else would be a better parent to her to fearing the "what ifs": *What if I died? Who could take care of her like I do? Who could possibly love her as much as I do?*

A little Mommy time

I was so depressed, I quit going to church. I made the excuse that it was too difficult to go with the kids. I didn't think anyone would know how to take care of them. David tried relentlessly every Sunday to get me out of the house and through the church doors. He knew that I needed our support system at church that we had relied on so heavily through the adoptions. Our church family had pulled me through many tough times and had a special way of lifting my spirits. I just got angrier at him for trying to put more responsibilities on my plate. Just the thought of having to get myself and the kids ready for church was more than I could handle.

The kids and I began travelling to Lubbock two and three times a week for therapy. I would wake the kids up early in the morning, somehow get them to potty while they were barely awake, and then load all three of my children in the car while they were still in their jammies. I had loaded a small cooler the night before with snacks, sippies, and a small breakfast. Once we got to the clinic, I would make everyone potty again, brush their teeth in the bathroom, and then dress them for the day. We would head home late that same day. I can't believe my precious two-year-olds—yes, I had two of them—were able to be such good travelers especially during potty training.

My poor baby, Brooke, had just turned two at the time. Her carefree life of freedom came to a startling halt as she now had to be confined to a car seat for hours upon hours a week. Maybe that is where she developed the amazing imagination she still enjoys today. She can play with one Polly Pocket for hours by herself in total contentment, yet, when ready, she shines as the baby of the family and puts on an award-winning talent show for any eager audience. She has the self-confidence of any Ivy League school graduate.

I graduated from college in Lubbock, and we had already been there many times for doctor appointments. I was very familiar with the town, and many of my dear friends still lived there. God used those long hours in the car to bring me close to him again. I began to find myself looking forward to those tiresome journeys. That was my much needed "me" time where I was forced to stop doing things around the house and actually spend time singing with my three sweet angels, playing road games, or simply talking to my Lord and Savior while they slept.

I developed a certain inner strength that I never knew I had thanks to that time with God and my babies. I also found myself thanking God for my blessings, my answered prayers. God also provided more miracles at Pediatric Therapy, Inc. I became really good friends with several of the ladies there, and before long, they invited me to a Bible study.

Since Ashley and Grant were both adopted by the state, they were fortunate enough to have Medicaid insurance as secondary coverage behind our personal insurance to cover all their therapies. The Medicaid coverage was initially assigned to them because of Ashley's medical needs with her vision, and Grant was diagnosed with asthma when he was a baby. No one knew at the time how much they would truly need Medicaid throughout the rest of their lives. What a blessing. God truly provides. There was not any way we would have been able to afford all of those road trips and therapies without that coverage, especially after the job change.

I also began using those trips to Lubbock to start interviewing and researching various schools since, by this point, David's new company said they were going to open an office there. We had to pull Ashley out of private school after the diagnosis. She had reached the point where we needed to utilize the resources in the public schools that the private schools were just not equipped to offer. This disappointed us as we pulled her out of the school where we had hoped she would graduate. She had been there for three years, and we were very fond of it.

Her last day of private kindergarten, I cried like a baby. Crying had become a routine occurrence, but I had too much pride to let anyone know how poorly I was handling it. I had to be strong like everyone thought. We had to put Ashley in the public school down from our house. It was a horrible experience.

In a two-month period, they completely ruined her self-esteem. They were not equipped, nor were they willing to work with Ashley. She has never been the same since. We decided quickly that we would pull her out and possibly just keep her home and start kindergarten over the next year in Lubbock.

I think I went to approximately nine different schools in Lubbock and the surrounding towns looking for just the right one to provide the best education and support for Ashley, Grant, and eventually Brooke. It was a difficult task since Ashley and Grant had totally different needs. Thankfully, I was not concerned with Brooke having special needs, but I wanted to make sure to find a place that would be appropriate for all three of them.

I was preparing myself to home school them, until one day I walked into Cooper Elementary and Ms. Cherie Nettles walked around the corner to introduce herself. Her beautiful, welcoming eyes and smile spoke priceless words, and her genuine spirit was evident. She was the assistant principal of the school, and she dropped everything for over an hour to show me the school, introduce me to teachers, and fully educate me on their philosophies of education. I knew without a doubt that we could now proudly call ourselves Cooper Pirates, but I also knew I needed to bring David and the kids to see if they felt what I felt.

We dropped in unannounced on Valentine's Day. We were running through town for a therapy session, and I simply was going to make an appointment for all of us to come back only to find that same friendly smile greeting me again. Although the halls were filled with happy children carrying pink and red balloons, flowers, candy, and parents were everywhere, Ms. Nettles again dropped everything and spent another hour or so with us rather than asking us to come back another day. That was it. I was on a mission to get our family to Lubbock by the end of spring break (only six weeks away) so Ashley could finish out the school year as a Cooper Pirate! Arrrrgh!

Within the next month, we listed and sold our home in Midland and moved into our camper—yes, a camper—until we found a home in Lubbock. Luckily we only had to live in the camper for six weeks. Living in the camper was not nearly as hard as leaving David behind in Midland until the new office in Lubbock could be established. The new office ended up being ready nine long, devastating months later. Marriage is difficult no matter what the circumstance. Long distance adds to that difficulty, but add raising three children under the age of five—two of which have special needs—to the mix, and that makes it almost impossible for a marriage to survive. Another factor to consider is that we adopted our three children in less than two years. We had only been married less than a year when Ashley entered our lives.

I read once that 80 percent of marriages fail raising

just one child with autism. That statistic is alarming. If we can make it, anyone can make it. We definitely have our problems, and there have been times where I wanted to wring his neck or send him to a far off country, but then I remember God. God's plan was for us to be together. God intended for David and me to raise all three of our children with all of their needs, no matter how big or how small. We gladly accepted the challenge, the blessing, and the honor.

Our "perfect" family

GIVE ME STRENGTH

The LORD is my strength and my song; he has
become my victory. He is my God, and I will praise
him; He is my father's God, and I will exalt him!

Exodus 15:2

The next three years after we moved to Lubbock went by
so quickly. I think I was just in survival mode. Each day
got more difficult. As my friends were beginning to enjoy
new activities and moments with their daughters, I was
just thanking God that I made it through the day with
mine. We began a halfhearted search for a new church
home. We missed that support from our previous church
home a great deal.

We seemed to have taken for granted the power of prayer
and the strength God provided throughout the three
years following the diagnosis. Instead, we chose to run on
fumes. I don't mean to sound as if I did not enjoy anything

in those three years, because I did. We have made wonderful friends in Lubbock. My children have blessed my life daily and have made an impact on many people. They are all so amazing. They make me smile. I can't imagine my life without any of them.

Although challenging, Ashley has an abundant amount of unconditional love, and she possesses a huge desire to please. Realizing these are great qualities to have, I have to put my guard up because at any minute all of that can change. If I don't have my guard up, I could get hurt and confused on how to parent her. I can't raise Ashley by emotion and with my heart like I was raised and like I raise the other two. I have to parent her knowing that what I am doing is in her best interest at all times. The minute she has an inch, she takes full advantage of it.

Ashley is so different than her brother and sister as far as learning by her mistakes. She continues to do the same thing over and over, even if it causes her or someone else pain. She will get in trouble for the same thing again and again. From what I understand, this is exactly why our justice system is so overloaded with criminals that continually make the same mistake. A majority of people in prison can be identified on the spectrum of fetal alcohol syndrome.

My love for Ashley is without judgment. I want the best for her. My heart hurts for her as my mind continuously strives to make the best decisions on her behalf in a very restricted environment.

Grant is such a little love. He is amazingly smart, funny, loving, affectionate, and handsome. He loves to love. He loves to learn. He loves to live. Although he has autism, he is extremely high functioning. He thrives in school and surprises his teachers and me often. He is a true joy to have in our family.

My Brooke is a little of Ashley, a little of Grant, a little of me, and a lot of answered prayers! She is the one that is my rock. She is my helper, my friend, my companion. And she loves life as well! I am getting to experience so many things through her. Some may think she is my favorite. I don't have a favorite. She just understands me more than anyone else on earth.

One night, Brooke and I were lying in bed together after saying our bedtime prayers when she suddenly sat up and started stroking my face with her sweet, tiny hands. She said, "Mommy, don't worry; when I grow up, I will take care of Ashley and Grant." I guess she not only understands me, but she understands them as well. She had an empathetic heart for their special needs at a very early age.

I feel so guilty sometimes for saying negative things about Ashley. It is certainly not because I do not love her, because I do. My grandmother used to say that hearts are full of pockets for everyone. Ashley has a large pocket of my heart that I hold very dear. I guess part of me thinks the more I talk about it, the more people will realize the severity of it and an end will come for this tragedy that is placed on helpless children throughout the world.

I don't consider the negative talk as being cruel or indifferent or even callous. I consider myself being very realistic when I talk about Ashley. For me, the more realistic I am, the better I understand her disability and the more I am able to assess her needs and follow through with getting help. I am very protective of Ashley. Sometimes, when another child is being cruel to Ashley, I am amazed at how childish I become. I can lash out with a zinger before I even know what hit me. How embarrassing is that? I hope they never tell their mommies!

All this said, my point is that there is no such thing as "over parenting" as far as Ashley is concerned. We have to be overprotective and overbearing. It is for her safety. Statistics show that less than ten percent of people with FAS are ever able to live on their own.

We have been told to get her into junior high and then focus on self-help skills more than academics. I say *whatever* to that. We are not giving up on her—ever! If she has to live with us forever, we are fully prepared for that. But we will never stop teaching her, as frustrating as that may be for her and for us. What we are teaching her now has to do with self-help and survival skills that will be necessary for her future.

Many people are aware that children with autism need constant supervision, and most parents do not get criticized for "over parenting." I believe this is because autism gets so much public awareness, and I am considerably appreciative for that. Therefore, it is not a secret how difficult raising a child with autism can be, but I will reiterate this right now—Grant is a breeze to raise compared to Ashley.

The difficulty in raising a child with FAS is what has motivated me to share our story with others. I want FAS to get as much recognition as autism because it is one hundred percent preventable!

There are a limited number of support groups for families dealing with FAS. I did attend one meeting shortly after we learned about Ashley's brain damage, and I had good intentions of getting actively involved, but after one meeting, I was just not strong enough emotionally to handle the hardcore truths the other more experienced families openly discussed. Maybe it was just bad timing.

Everyone talked about the unimaginable difficulties, describing the teenage years as a living hell. The older, more seasoned parents were still raising their children who were in their twenties and thirties. The stories were horrible. The warnings were unbelievable. At the time, I did not want to listen. Their stories did not pertain to our family. Reality for me was that we were going to be one of the ten percent success stories that had a happy ending. What I personally needed was to hear the good along with the bad. I hope my story reflects both.

Another reason I want to get this story out is because a lot of mothers are told by their doctors that it is okay to drink wine or beer conservatively and it will not harm the baby. That is completely untrue. I want to reemphasize that one single drink could harm a baby while still in the womb. Each instance totally depends on how the baby, not the mother, metabolizes the alcohol.

Many children who have been diagnosed are children who are adopted. It is more difficult for children who are with their biological mothers to get diagnosed. I can only imagine how difficult it would be as a birthmother to realize the permanent damage they caused their child because they chose to drink during pregnancy. That does not necessarily mean they are bad mothers or neglectful mothers. I hope they were just uneducated just like the doctors who told them it was okay to drink in the first place.

Any doctor who has advised women that it is okay to have a glass of wine here and there during pregnancy, should get on his hands and knees and ask for God's forgiveness. The doctor should use the rare opportunity he has been given to train the mother for nine months on how to physically protect her unborn child that God has graciously created in her womb.

My commitment to raising awareness and educating people on FAS is not just limited to writing this book. I have attempted to create local and national awareness by contacting well-known public figures. A couple of years ago, for instance, I began consistently contacting *The Oprah Winfrey Show* to share my story. I wanted to encourage her to do an hour on FAS because she has done several shows on autism. She could help to educate other "mothers-to-be" about the dangers of drinking while pregnant. I never received a reply. I am sure she receives millions of stories. I told her it would be easier for me to raise ten more children with autism like my son, Grant, than one more child with FAS.

Oprah is not the only show I have contacted. I have sent e-mails regarding our story to *Dr. Phil, The Doctors,* 60 *Minutes,* NBC, CBS, ABC, TLC, and Discover Networks. I have yet to receive a reply from anyone. The lack of response only solidifies my concerns that people truly are unknowing of this terrible, preventable, leading cause of brain abnormalities in the United States.

Fortunately, the local news station did an interview on Ashley and ran a short segment on the evening news. The local newspaper also came to our home to interview us and wrote an article in the *Lubbock Avalanche Journal.* Ashley considers herself famous due to the local attention.

CHALLENGED BY THE CHARACTERISTICS

Dear brothers and sisters, whenever trouble comes your way, let it be an opportunity for joy. For when your faith is tested, your endurance has a chance to grow. So let it grow, for when your endurance is fully developed, you will be strong in character and ready for anything. If you need wisdom—if you want to know what God wants you to do—ask him, and he will gladly tell you. He will not resent your asking. But when you ask him, be sure that you really expect him to answer, for a doubtful mind is as unsettled as a wave of the sea that is driven and tossed by the wind.

James 1: 2–6

James is one of my all time favorite books in the Bible. Not once, not twice, not even three times, but numerous times I have been led to this book to get me through some of the toughest times in my life. In this chapter, I have included many of the challenges Ashley faces on any given day. Many of these challenges have been briefly mentioned throughout the book, but my main goal is to make sure to completely educate people on what we experience. I am not a professional, but I feel it is imperative to share what we personally face. Some children with FAS may experience a few but not all of these characteristics, and then I am sure there are other characteristics of FAS that I have not mentioned. I want others to be aware of the things that they are exposing their unborn miracles to each time they take a sip of an alcoholic beverage during pregnancy. I can't understand why anyone would want to take the risk unless they are not informed that it is actually a risk!

INSPIRED BY OTHERS' THOUGHTS AND ACTIONS

I mentioned earlier that Ashley does not learn by her mistakes or experiences. My hairdresser asked me the other day if I thought Ashley took advantage of her illness. I had never really thought about that. I stay so amazed at the things she does not understand that sometimes I don't appreciate the things she does understand. There are a few people whom Ashley will obey no matter what her mood is, and then there are a few people that Ashley is so mean, hateful, and defiant to that I often challenge her thinking, knowing that she seems capable of controlling her thoughts and actions at times.

After my hairdresser said that, I thought to myself, *You know, I could probably tell Ashley that I got a phone call and the doctor said she was all better. She could then act and participate in activities just like other children her age.* I know I could never actually do that to her, but as mean as that sounds, it would probably work … for a while. I know it would not make a difference in her capabilities physically, mentally, and academically, but I truly wonder if it would make a difference in her behavior.

This realization is so difficult to grasp and is probably one of the most terrifying issues regarding her condition. Ashley is easily influenced and persuaded by others. She believes anything she is told if she can remember it. We are supposed to keep her very guarded once she hits those anticipated teenage years.

A minor example of Ashley being influenced by others has to do with blowing her nose. She may see someone blow his nose, so she blows her nose. Yet when it is obvious that she needs to blow her nose because she is sniffling, stuffy, or has a runny nose, it never occurs to her to do something about it without someone giving her a cue to do so. Although I gave an example that would not be detrimental to Ashley's health or safety, it does indicate how easily influenced she is.

Individuals with FAS are very susceptible to drugs, alcohol abuse, theft, and other illegal activities. "Friends" will persuade them to do something in return for friendship or favors, and people like Ashley will gladly carry out the dirty job for others with no clue about the consequences. My fears are being confirmed as Ashley is continuously drawn to the bully. It does not seem to matter to her how many times the bully will intentionally hurt Ashley, she goes right back in for more.

It is very common for people with FAS to not only lose their virginity early, but to be very promiscuous as well. They think they are in love. They think people will love them or they will be accepted by others. They also realize it might be something that feels good, and it takes away the pain that they experience but don't truly understand where that pain is coming from. The reality is she could get pregnant. This poor child could actually have a child of her own. What would we do then?

Experiencing these good feelings as opposed to the feelings that overpower them most of the time are the very same reasons that these innocent angels also experiment with drugs and alcohol. They are already predisposed for possible alcoholic traits considering their birthmothers may have been alcoholics, but now they are faced with genetics and society without the ability to fully comprehend either one.

ANXIETY

Friends have always given me a hard time about being a *fraidy* cat. I have to admit, I do get scared easily, but the older I get, the more secure I am knowing that I am safe with God as my protector. I can't imagine going through life like Ashley. She is absolutely uncomfortable in her own skin. She jumps and yells all the time like people are "spooking" her on purpose. Sometimes I wonder if it is her vision. I can reach up to push my hair out of my face, and she dodges me like I am either going to hit her or something is going to fall down on her. I often wonder if that is some sort of memory flash from her past as well. It's almost like she can't judge what is happening out of the corner of her eye, or maybe she is just that jumpy.

Her anxiety can be difficult when she is faced with anything new. Lots of structure helps reduce some of Ashley's anxiety. But when (not if) anything changes, we had better be prepared. She is incredibly shy and fears anything that has to do with socialization. At times, we have to physically pick her up and carry her into a new environment. Ashley starts rubbing her hands together like she is making a snake out of Play-Doh. She scrunches up her face because she is rubbing so hard and so fast.

If that coping mechanism doesn't work, she will start pinching her legs or gripping onto something like she is holding on for dear life while she holds her breath. At times, she has squeezed her neck so tightly that she will stop herself from breathing. Afterwards, she actually has bruises and broken blood vessels.

Her skin is very sensitive, and it does not take much to leave a mark. I am in constant fear of what she could actually do to herself due to her anxiety. In some instances, Ashley handles the anxiety in a totally different manner. Instead of physical indicators, I have to watch for a sense of calmness which is very unusual. If Ashley is very quiet and still, she is usually worrying about something.

Recently, her choir class at church was preparing for a concert of sorts. They mailed out invitations and had many extra practices. Ashley voiced her excitement. She loved choir and could not wait to invite her friends. The closer the concert became, the more intensified her anxiety became. She started acting out in school by yelling at the teacher, refusing to do her work, tearing up things at home and school, *including* her glasses that we just bought. She started talking about how nervous she was about the concert. We finally decided that is was just not a good idea for her to participate. We did not want her to think we were punishing her, but it became a concern for her health. She was very upset and cried inconsolably for about five minutes when we told her, and then it was like the weight of the world was lifted off her shoulders. She was free to be Ashley again with no worries in the world—for the moment anyway.

We have realized that the longer she has to prepare for a big event, the more difficult it is. Most kids handle things better with lots of preparation and information. Not Ashley. The more she knows, the more she has to worry about.

The decision to withhold her from the choir concert was really difficult for David as well. He made the comment that it just wasn't fair to her to not let her do the things that normal kids do. I had to remind him that her normal is not the same as someone else's normal.

All of a sudden I got a flashback from seven years ago when I attempted to put Ashley into ballet and she threw such a tantrum on the day the parents watched. I was the one ashamed and embarrassed. I thought, *What if we let her do it, and right in the middle of the performance with a completely full sanctuary, Ashley fell apart. What if she started screaming, crying, flapping her hands, and hyperventilating? Would it ruin the performance that they worked so hard for? Would anyone but me even notice Ashley in that huge crowd? Would it be good for her?*

Ashley is involved in a special needs competitive cheer team and a special needs dance class. Both classes have teachers who have experience working with children with special needs, so their focus is to help children through social situations by reducing performance anxiety. These types of classes help with physical strength, coordination, memory, and promote social interaction.

Another nervous habit she developed was pulling out her hair and wadding it into balls. She rubs her hands together rapidly when she gets nervous, and having something small to roll between her hands seems to be even better. I can't tell you how many of those disgusting little hairballs I would find all over the house. Her favorite spots to hide the hair balls were in her pillowcase and under her bed.

She would eat them sometimes and stuff them in her ears or up her nose. Thank goodness she somehow got over that habit. I had to finally tell her that the doctors might have to operate on her if she kept eating her hair-balls. There is actually a medical term for pulling your hair called *Trichotillomania*.

Once she stopped pulling her hair, she started sticking stuffed animal stuffing and tissue paper in her ears and up her nose. The last of many visits to the doctor's office to dig two huge cotton-ball size mounds of stuffing out of her nose actually seemed to cure that. She tends to get stuffed animals from family at Christmas even though I have asked them not to give her stuffed animals or dolls. I have requested this not out of meanness but to eliminate a possible accident.

For a while, she wasn't even allowed to sleep with a pillow because she would pull the stuffing out of it as well. The solution I have found that works best is to cover her pillow in four pillowcases, closing up both entrances to the actual pillow not once but twice. I attempted to ratio-nalize why Ashley chose to stuff things up her nose and in her ears. I decided it was due to sensory overload. Maybe she was trying to drown out sounds and smells.

Anxiety overcomes Ashley during storms as well. When we first moved to Lubbock, it seemed like there were thunderstorm warnings and tornado warnings nightly. Ashley would hide in her closet under her clothes. The minute the television alert would sound, it was like a beacon had gone off, and Ashley would run to see if the storm was going to get us and end it all. During those times was when Ashley developed a new way to handle the stress. She started pulling her own teeth. The teeth were not even loose, I might add. She pulled her first four teeth during panic attacks. I asked her if it hurt since they were not even loose, and she gave me the reassurance that "No, it did not hurt; it just made a weird crunching noise."

Some of her anxiety is the result of paranoia. She can make herself literally ill just by worrying over the smallest things such as what time of day it is, what day of the week it is, or if we turned the car in the right direction to get to where we are going. There are times when she is overwhelmed by the fear of running out of groceries or running out of gas. Ashley gets concerned that David or I will forget to pick her up from school or from an activity, and she will intentionally wet herself or make herself throw-up or just say she is sick so the teacher will have to call us.

We have had three different experiences with Ashley in retail stores when they are about to close. Once she hears the announcement that the store will be closing in "five minutes" she starts crying and eventually stops breathing. We learned quickly that Ashley cannot go shopping in the evening. She can't explain what scares her so badly, but I think she fears we will be locked in the store and cannot get out. We have tried to prepare her for times like that and explain to her what we would do if the store closed, but she cannot understand.

Sporting her new self-inflicted grin

PACING

Anxiety has a lot to do with Ashley pacing or walking uncontrollably without any purpose and without any intention of stopping, but it is also very common with children with special needs specifically related to brain abnormalities. I have been known to tell Ashley that she is wearing a hole in my carpet. In our last house, she could walk circles from one end of the house around the kitchen island to the other end of the house repeatedly. As she walked, she swung her arms, wringing her hands, and talked indistinctly. Each round she hit something new whether it was her hand, wrist, toe, or the new lamp I just bought and sat proudly in the perfect spot on the sofa table.

The pacing is due to boredom, anxiety, and sometimes she is lost. I don't understand the pacing, and it drives me absolutely crazy. I have told her to go find something to do, which completely throws her for a loop because to her pacing uncontrollably is doing something. If that doesn't work, I tell her to "go perch" somewhere. Not very nice, I know. But that usually gets her to sit down and watch TV. If that does not work, I have to be very specific and tell her to go sit in the pink chair in her room and watch TV.

I think I mentioned before that she does not really get the whole concept of toys. She does not know how to constructively entertain herself. She doesn't know how to play with them, and she doesn't really enjoy sitting down to read. Every now and then I can get her to sit at the table and color, but before I know it, she has knocked over the box of crayons, written all over herself, or she has chosen the dull red crayon as a snack. I hate to always put her in front of the TV, but if I need to get a few things done and I can't watch her much less deal with the pacing, then TV is the best solution for the both of us

Just having fun

DESTRUCTIVENESS

Where do I even start with this one? I think one reason Ashley's destructive behavior bothers me so badly is because I am the complete opposite. I take very good care of my things, not to mention the respect I have for other people's property. The first thing that comes to mind that Ashley destroyed is her bedding. When Ashley turned three, we decided to go all out and decorate her room with custom bedding. We did not get to do this for her nursery since she was older when we got her. She was in between a nursery and a "big girl" room. This was our chance. The fabrics we chose were a pink and green plaid, pink toile, hot pink leopard, and a green and pink floral. Oh my gosh! It was to die for. The comforter was a duvet comforter with plaid, fabric-covered buttons down each side rather than across the top.

Being the overprotective mom that I am, I purposely designed it this way so the buttons would not be near her face. I wanted to prevent any possible choking hazard. What did she do? She pulled every one of them off within the next year and chewed them up. I would find them in random places looking like they had been through one of those penny-flattening machines at Six Flags. I would ask her what happened, and she would just look at me and say, "I don't know." That's the standard answer to date. I had to throw away the duvet. I left the down comforter on her bed for a while until I realized that all the feathers under her bed were thankfully not from a dead bird she found in the yard but from the remnants of her beautiful bedding. I had to toss that and resort to a quilt without any stuffing. Shortly after I placed the quilt on her bed, I started finding random balls of string throughout the house, only to discover she was pulling the thread from the pieced quilt.

Finally, I found what I considered a durable throw quilt at Target, and voila, problem solved, except for the fact that nothing matches in her room now, but she does not notice things like that.

Her beautiful bedding

Her bedding is not a necessity, but her glasses are. Ashley breaks her glasses often. It is not uncommon to find a pair chewed up. One time I noticed tons of scratches on the lenses. I assumed she had skidded across the parking lot on her face or something—a vision I have seen far too many times. A far scarier vision was in store for me. Ashley found a pushpin on the floor of her classroom, and she proceeded to scratch up her lenses with the pin while they were on!

As weak as her vision is, she doesn't understand why she wears glasses. She even forgets to put them on and at times wears them upside down. She gets them confused with sunglasses. She thinks she wears glasses because the sun or lights are too bright. Ashley has very little pigmentation, if any, behind her eyes, which makes her very sensitive to sunlight. Sunglasses would help tremendously with the sensitivity, but again, she forgets to wear them, doesn't recognize she needs them, or destroys them.

On a recent trip to Dallas, we took our new car with freshly tinted windows. David always tints the windows. He thinks we are safer, but I think he just likes the look. We put Ashley in the very back. She can't sit by either one of the kids because she constantly bothers them.

When I looked back to tell everyone something, I noticed something looked very wrong with the tint job. After inspecting it a little closer, I realized it had been etched in random mosaic patterns all over the entire window. I asked Ashley what happened, and, of course, she said, "I don't know." Then I found the evidence. The metal part of her clip was sitting in the cup holder. It was a hair clip that had a metal spring that held both pieces together. Ashley broke the clip, removed the metal spring, and used it to destroy our window.

Once we pointed out that we knew exactly what she did, she changed the common response of "I don't know" to the next anticipated response of "I didn't do it. I promise." The evidence was there. We knew she did it. We knew how she did it. Case closed. Ashley, however, has never fessed up to it to this day.

Several months later, I had a travel bag in the backseat which had a bottle of children's nail polish in it. I picked up Ashley from school, and we went straight home. When I was getting the kids out of the car, I noticed a polka dotted window where Ashley was sitting. She had dotted the window with nail polish and left the bottle in her seat.

Thank goodness she put the lid back on. I was furious and asked her what on earth she was thinking, and she said in a very calm voice, "I didn't do that." There was no arguing with her. I could tell by the look in her eye that she was completely convinced that she really did not do it. I guess that was my fault; I know now that I have to always be thinking ahead of time, and I should have never put her in the car without moving everything out of her reach, but I knew she would just be in the car less than five minutes.

She ruins everything she touches. Granted, I know it is not always on purpose, but the point is it is *always* happening. She can't stop. She is not allowed in my room, Grant's room, or Brooke's room without asking. Ashley's number one rule at the house is, "If it's not yours, do not touch it." I can't say it works one hundred percent of the time, but I can use that rule when she does break something to remind her of why she should not play with other people's property.

Ashley does not only destroy things at home. Unfortunately, this applies to school property as well. One time in kindergarten, she took a permanent marker and drew a straight line all the way down the wall of her classroom.

This behavior makes it very difficult to take her with us when we visit friend's houses. I can't ask them to put everything up, and even if I could, she would still find something that would spark her interest and she would break it. One time we were at my cousin's house, and Ashley broke open a collector box of shells and ruined the box.

I have found that it helps me to send Ashley to daycare after school and during the summer. I am a better mother to her if I get breaks from having to constantly watch her to make sure she is not destroying something. I finally found a daycare that seemed to understand how serious Ashley's disability is.

Things were going fairly well and then I got the dreaded call from the school. During rest time, Ashley found a black dry erase marker. She hid under her blanket and proceeded to color her entire face, eyebrows, teeth, tops and bottoms of both of her hands and feet as well as her pony tail before anyone ever noticed. It took days for it to all wash off. I was concerned about the toxins that had to be absorbed in her body from the marker.

I know that was not the first time she had destroyed something that was dangerous to her health. One time, I was dusting Ashley's room, and I noticed all the corners of her furniture were raw. The paint and the stain were worn off, and they even looked like they had been sanded into a new edge. I decided to keep a closer eye on her for the next few days to see what in the world she could have done to them. Come to find out she was gnawing on them. She would move from corner to corner, moving her teeth back and forth to create a human saw. Of course, the next thought that came to mind was lead poisoning. I decided to take her to the doctor by this point for blood tests to see if she had ingested toxins at any time.

Another time, I was making her bed and found a flashlight from Christmas. It was rusted, gooey and wet. The top was off. She had chewed up the batteries! Back to the doctor we went for another test to see if she had ingested anything. I spend so much time in the doctor's office with her because of these weird destructive behaviors. I guess some of my decisions to "ground" her from certain objects or events are not only because of her safety but because of time. I just can't spend four or more hours a week in the doctor's office with her fixing something that could have been prevented.

Christmas is very difficult for her. Grant and Brooke

have identified their favorite things to collect and play with by now. I can go shopping on any given day and find something that I know they will love and cherish. Ashley, on the other hand, is a different story. I can't really buy her toys, and it's very difficult to take her shopping to find something she would enjoy because she destroys so many things in the store by simply handling them or running into things. It is also difficult to keep up with her because she gets focused on other things and wanders off.

She could care less about clothes or girly things like purses and jewelry. She does like to color, but she will sit down and go through an entire book and box of crayons or markers in about thirty minutes, and then she is bored again and acts up. On Christmas mornings, after she unwraps her gifts, she destroys or loses half of them by noon and wonders what she can do the rest of the day.

SAFETY

Ashley's destructive behavior causes great concern for her safety. Because of some of her uncontrollable habits, she does not have very many things in her room. Not that we won't buy them for her, but she either breaks the one we buy within minutes after opening it, she loses it, or she just simply cannot find anything at the store that she really likes or understands enough to buy.

One time, when Ashley was about four, I had one of those weird mommy feelings, so I walked in her room in the middle of the night to check on her. She had been playing with a small stuffed animal that had a strap on it. Somehow she had put her hand through the strap and twisted it so many times that it was in knots around her wrist. Her hand was hanging off the bed, and the stuffed toy was hanging off her wrist. She was sound asleep. I was fearful, of course, of the circulation being cut off, so I immediately started twisting until I could finally slip her hand out. There was a deep indention all the way around her wrist, and the coloring was a little off. I massaged her hand for a few minutes to get circulation going again. She never woke up.

Not only are there few things in her room; I have also put forth a lot of effort to keep it somewhat clean. There are many pictures of friends and family so she can focus on the people who love her so much. She loves having the pictures in her room, but I have to pay close attention to the glass on some of the pictures because she has broken the glass out before. I also have to make sure none of the pictures are missing on the walls, because she pulls the nails out of the walls to scratch furniture and scratch herself. I would love to have a bulletin board in her room to display her accomplishments, but she tends to put thumbtacks and magnets in her mouth. She asked for a desk in her room, and I thought that was a good idea. It would provide a quiet, "get away" place for her. Unfortunately, I cannot put pencils, pens, or scissors in the desk for her to enjoy.

In her room, she has two huge windows that overlook beautiful landscaping in the front yard. I strategically placed her trunk in front of those windows. I told her she could sit on it to look outside, but the real reason I put it there and filled it with heavy trophies is so she could not move it and lean out the window. I know some people might think I suffer from paranoia, but I have to constantly be paranoid about the things she might do because she has done so many unimaginable things in the past.

EATING HABITS

It is hard to know if Ashley's eating challenges are due to FAS or if it is a consequence of the neglect she endured her first year of life. Children with FAS do have some eating difficulties, so I think Ashley got a double-whammy.

She attended feeding therapy for almost two years. Feeding therapy focused on three main goals. First, they tried to get her to take small bites in order to chew her food. She prefers to swallow her food without chewing, which scares me to death thinking she is going to choke. She has very weak, undeveloped muscles in her jaw and mouth, so chewing literally wears her out. It is like exercise to her. It is just easier for her to stick the whole thing in her mouth and swallow it. Weak muscles are another common factor in FAS. In Ashley's case, she not only suffers from brain damage, but she also has joint, muscle, and nerve damage which all affect her eating.

Second, they tried to teach her to take three sips of a drink at a time. Ashley still has issues with milk, and I can only imagine how unappealing milk would be if I drank diluted, rancid milk for days on end. Ashley prefers Silk brand vanilla soymilk. We actually started her on Silk after she first started living with us. We noticed that she spit up a lot after drinking milk or milk products. We thought maybe it was an allergic reaction, so we started her on Silk, which reduced the spit-up unless she consumed it too quickly or consumed too much.

Ashley can down a jug of water or Silk in two seconds flat. Evidently her brain does not tell her when to stop or when she is full. We pray every day she never tries alcohol! Not only is it in her genes to love alcohol, it is also very common for FAS children to seek an addiction. I'm afraid

Ashley would win every keg contest, because she would not stop until the keg was empty.

Finally, the feeding therapist taught her to try various foods in regard to the look, smell, texture, or temperature of the food. Now she is very compliant with trying new foods.

We have seen a pediatric gastroenterologist who told us Ashley did not have any medical condition such as reflux or any other type of disorder that would cause her to spit-up, but it was highly probable that the spit-up had to do with subconscious issues she faced from her infancy. She might have actually remembered the feelings of not having food and, therefore, ate so quickly or so much that it created the reaction of vomiting. There was also the possibility that she created that survival technique as an infant for attention. There were several different times in her adoption file where her birthmother *dropped* Ashley off at the nearest hospital because of spitting up. Maybe Ashley discovered even at the earliest age that if she spit up, someone would notice her and take care of her. Now the urge to drink large amounts of anything quickly and then vomiting is an uncontrollable habit that is impossible to break. Sometimes I can tell she has something in her mouth. When I ask her what she is eating, she will show me, and it's vomit!

All I ever hear is how mealtime is one of the most important times of the day for a family to bond. Whatever! For us, it has always been one of the most stressful times. This is another commonality of families who have children with special needs. We do have some enjoyable meals, but it has been a long journey getting there. For the most part, our meals consist of reminding Ashley to chew with her mouth closed so food doesn't fall out. It is difficult for any of us to sit across from her.

It sounds so cruel to talk about it like this. I am sorry if it sounds like I am heartless. Sometimes I feel heartless. I don't mean to be cruel. I just get frustrated. I know it is not her fault, but I am not going to give up trying to teach her manners at the table. As far as eating fast and messy, I remind myself of what the gastroenterologist said regarding submersed feelings from when she was in the homeless shelter.

The way that Ashley eats is not the only challenge during mealtime. The lack of focus and coordination also play a major part. We are usually cleaning up something that she has spilled, which sometimes includes herself. Yes, sometimes it is actually Ashley that we are cleaning up off the floor. She can't sit still in her chair, so it is not unusual for her to actually fall out of her chair or tip the chair over with her in it.

SELF-AWARENESS

We continue to help Ashley with personal hygiene. She is so unaware of her body that she can't tell when her clothes are on correctly. She had to start wearing a bra at age seven because she started developing breasts a little early. No one knows exactly why she developed breasts at that age, but it is assumed it might be due to all of the medicines she has been on. Some children with FAS do develop early, which is very scary because most are not able to handle some aspects of puberty such as their menstrual cycle.

As far as her bra is concerned, she will put it on backward, upside down, or inside out and never think twice about it. She will wear her panties all day long with two legs in one hole and never even realize it is uncomfortable, much less cutting the circulation off her legs. I can't tell you how many times she has walked out of her room with her swimsuit on backward or her undershirt over her top shirt. There have been times she's put her leggings on outside of her shorts.

She is still completely oblivious if her face is dirty or her clothes are torn. She doesn't care. I keep wipes in the car at all times. The minute Ashley gets in the car after school, I have to tell her to clean her face and hands. I can usually guess what she ate for lunch simply by looking at the remnants of lunch on her cheeks, mouth, and clothing. Ashley struggles with sensory issues, so I would think the sticky or wet substance stuck to her face would drive her crazy.

PERSONAL HYGIENE

I have tried to teach her to bathe herself, and her hands just can't maneuver in a way to wash her hair. I will put the soap on the rag, and I let her do the rest, but I have to watch. If I don't squirt the soap on the rag, then she will pour the entire bottle in the tub in one sitting. She can't brush her own hair, and she really doesn't care if it is brushed or not. Brushing her hair is torturous to her. She thinks we are pulling her hair and abusing her. The sound of the blow dryer sends her over the edge. However, she doesn't quite make as big of a deal out of it if the hairdresser is doing it instead of me. She struggles with wiping her bottom as well. I have had to let go of that some because Super Nanny says, "Practice makes perfect."

MEMORY

Short-term memory loss is one of the biggest challenges with FAS. It affects everything they do from school work, learning from the mistakes and being able to function in their daily routine. There are days where she cannot even find her way to her own bathroom because she gets confused as to where she is in the house. It is not uncommon to find her walking in closets looking for a common area in the house.

This is a great concern when we are in public places. Ashley easily gets lost. The most difficult part is that if she were to get lost and someone were to ask her if she needed help, she would have trouble getting her thoughts organized and have trouble reducing her anxiety level enough to let them know how to help. It is of constant stress on me as well. I am always worried about her. I wonder if she will find her way to her classroom or if she will even find her way back to me after school. I have tried to teach her our phone number and our address. Some days she will remember, and some days she will not.

One time, we asked everyone to go get in the car, which was parked in the garage. We got in the car to leave, and Ashley was not in there. We found her in our master closet, which is located on the opposite side of the house through our master bedroom and through our master bathroom. She said she was still looking for the garage. Then another time we went to a birthday party at a friend's house. She had never been there before. She came up to me laughing and said, "Mommy, this house is like our house. I can't find my way anywhere."

Forgetting how to get to her room is not dangerous, but it certainly causes concern when I relate it to other areas of life. For instance, Ashley has had swimming lessons every summer since she was two. Each summer it is like we are starting all over. You can almost guarantee that at least one sun-loving lifeguard is going to make that life-saving plunge into the ice cold water to rescue my blue-eyed little fish. Ashley is very capable of jumping off the diving board and getting safely to the side on a good day. On a not-so-good day, Ashley is more likely to flash a huge smile, wave a wobbly hand at me, yelling, "Hi, Mommy!" like she saw me for the first time, and then jump in the water, completely forgetting what to do next as she sinks to the bottom of the pool.

I heard another parent talking one time. Their son was in his thirties and had FAS. They built a garage apartment behind their house for him to live in. They had to take out the oven because he would forget to turn it off, and they were afraid of a fire. I fear that for Ashley's future. Even now, she will walk away from the sink after brushing her teeth and leave the water running. Every morning, *every* morning, she gets out of the car for school and forgets to shut the door.

CONFUSION

The ability to distinguish reality from fantasy is a difficult concept for her to grasp, which could explain the never-ending lies she tells. In her mind, I truly think she thinks she is telling the truth. At times, I know she is going to lie because she can. Lying is one of the only things in her life that she has complete ownership and complete control of. Just imagine going through life completely out of control, feeling like you are in a car spinning in circles, and you can't do anything to make it stop and are just waiting for it to collide into another obstacle.

I remember one time when I was a teenager going to the carnival with a girlfriend of mine. We got on the tilt-a-whirl. The guy that was in charge of our ride evidently decided to take a break. We were screaming for someone to stop the ride. Once we finally got off, we were so sick, we just wanted to end the day and go home. We gave up. We sat down on the curb and waited, completely nauseous, for my friend's mom to come get us. That uncontrollable, nauseous feeling must be what Ashley feels like most days.

As with all children with brain abnormalities, Ashley suffers from constant confusion, whether it relates to the temperature outside or life and death. She can literally start sweating if it is twenty degrees outside and the sun is shining. In her mind, she thinks because the sun is shining, it must be hot.

One time, I caught her lying by her bedroom door. She said she was hot and she needed air. I explained to her that she was lying under the return air vent. The coolest place in her room is in her bed where her air conditioning vent was located. I explained to her that the cool air comes from that vent. A couple of days later, I went to tuck her in bed and she was shivering. I asked her what was wrong, and she said that because I moved her vent over her bed, she gets cold. She was convinced there was a change. Nothing had changed, including the temperature of her room.

Ashley wears her huge coat all the time; it is very comforting to her like a baby blanket in a sense. She wears it when it is 114 degrees outside with the west Texas wind blowing. Since the wind is blowing, she thinks it is cold outside.

There are a couple of other things that come to mind when discussing the confusion that Ashley experiences. She is very rough. She tries to tickle or hug us, and she actually hurts us. It is not on purpose, but to her, she is being gentle. She is the exact opposite with other things.

If we barely touch her, she thinks we have hurt her badly. I can pretty much guarantee she will fall at least once or run into something from the minute she wakes up until she steps foot in her classroom. She can trip over a curb and face-plant into the asphalt, jump up, and say, "I'm okay." Yet, a little pinch on the leg can cause her to have convulsions on the floor due to the pain.

Ashley has had the opportunity to experience everything her little life has to offer once we got our hands on her. She has been introduced to many friends in church, and we enrolled her in a private Christian preschool. She struggled relating to friends and chose to play with imaginary friends over real ones.

For a while, we thought it was fun to take two of her imaginary friends, Iyla and Alley, everywhere we went. I know of several friends who had an imaginary Alley living in their homes. Could Alley actually be real—an angel from heaven sent down to entertain and possibly protect so many little girls?

By now, Ashley should have outgrown the imaginary friends, but seven years later, I am just glad we don't have to pay for them when we go out to eat or when we go on vacation. Alley did not last as long as Iyla and two others, Tawnee and Loloa, (I assume that is how they are spelled) but Ashley has been friends with them for quite a while. Iyla tends to be her best friend. She does not talk about the other two as much. She doesn't want to share them with us or anyone at school because she says they are her friends.

Along with the imaginary friends are the voices that go along with them. Ashley says she hears voices in the middle of the night and people tapping her on the shoulder. We have not been able to determine if this is her imagination or if she really hears these voices. I know one thing: it is very evident on days that her "friends" were in the room keeping her awake during bedtime because the minute her feet hit the floor, she is ready to fight. When she doesn't sleep, she is a bear to deal with. She says Iyla comes to her room in the middle of the night and wakes her up, asks to sleep with her, and then takes all the covers.

I probably need to point out that imaginary friends are not a common characteristic of FAS specifically but there is some evidence that they are common in certain types of irregular brain development. This could also be an underlying trait of another disorder that has yet to be revealed.

I received a call from a parent of a child in Ashley's class one time. The parent was very concerned and wanted to know if she could help us in any way. Completely confused, I asked her why she thought we needed help. She said she heard that Ashley and her father were in a car wreck. Ashley had told some friends that she and her dad were in a car wreck and they were not wearing their seatbelts. According to Ashley, the truck flipped over into some bushes. A few days later, Ashley told me that her best friend's dad was killed in a car accident. Neither of the two stories was true. I can only assume that she saw or heard bits and pieces of a television show and somehow thought it happened to us personally.

I honestly do not think she was just making up stories. She doesn't have that kind of imagination. When I tried to talk to her about it, she just stared at me with a dazed look, and I could not determine if the look meant I did not know what I was talking about, she did not know what I was talking about, or she could not believe that I did not think the wreck really happened. No matter what the look meant, every word I said to her went in one ear, and who knows where they ended up.

Another time, she got in the car after school, and I could tell she was very sad. I asked her what was wrong, and she said, "Oh, I am just still sad my best friend's dad died when that stingray stuck him in the heart. I really miss him a lot." I knew she was talking about the crocodile hunter, Steve Irwin's death. She had never met him, never talked to him, and actually never even saw his show, but to her, she lost someone very important in her life. I think just hearing it on the news and learning he had a daughter made her feel close to him.

Halloween is always a huge dilemma around here. Ashley gets completely freaked out seeing everyone in a costume. It doesn't matter if the costume is supposed to be scary or friendly, she gets confused on who the person really is. We tried dressing her up the first two years we had her. Before we ever left the house, she would start screaming.

The following year, we had completely decided to give up the holiday all together, when she told us she wanted to be "Super Bingo." I have no idea where she came up with the idea or name. She said Super Bingo was red and black. I waited until the last possible minute to get the costume ready because I figured she would change her mind and lose the courage to go trick or treating. Finally, I ran to Target and grabbed a full body, black velvet leotard, a red cape and some face paint.

I painted a big SB on the chest of the leotard and painted the cutest red and black mask on her face. Then I put her hair in dog ears with two huge red bows. She looked so cute. We loaded Ashley and the babies up in the car and decided we would just go to one or two friend's houses. We pulled up to the first friend's house and Ashley saw people walking up and down the street, and she started screaming, crying, and hid on the floorboard. We never even got out of the car.

Finally, this past year, when she was eight, she got the courage to go to the church for Halloween. She said she wanted to be Ashley Tisdale from the Disney movie *High School Musical*. I bought the outfit, and for the very first time, all three kids actually trick or treated. She wore sunglasses, which I think helped her feel hidden. She showed a few of her anxious behaviors but for the most part, handled it well. When we got in the car, she made the comment that she could not believe so many people thought she was Ashley Taylor, herself, rather than Ashley Tisdale, the star. To her, once she put on the costume, she really was a different person. No wonder she got so scared at all the other people dressed up for so many years. She could not distinguish between the real character and the character in a costume.

LYING

Lying is very common with almost all children with FAS. They lie about anything and everything. It is their way of having control on their uncontrollable lives. We don't necessarily find humor in Ashley's lies. We find it very frustrating and very concerning. We have talked until we are blue in the face trying to get her to realize how important the truth is. We have used every example we know of from the Bible and God's commandments to the fact that she could end up in jail.

Ashley lies about the smallest things to the largest things and everything in between. We have tried everything from grounding her, taking away privileges, pulling up to the police station, washing her mouth out with soap, putting pepper juice on her tongue (we were taught this in a parenting class), to moving up bedtime. The Bible says that those who lie, their days will be cut short. Well, if she goes to bed early, then at least we are saving her from the ability to lie about anything else.

We are so scared she will tell some humdinger to the wrong person and they will believe her. She is very convincing. Like I said, we don't find humor in her lies, but I do want to share this one story because it not only portrays humor, but it also demonstrates how convincing she is and how convinced she is that she is telling the truth. Sometimes I wonder if she actually knows she is lying or if, in her world, what comes out of her mouth is how she perceives it.

Anyway, last year I got an e-mail from her teacher in the middle of the day. She informed me that Ashley had cut her hair *again* at school, but this time she got a substantial amount and her bangs were pretty spiky. Most moms expect to get news like this at least once early on in school, but Ashley was in second grade. Give me a break. I was fuming. Remember, I mentioned that Ashley does not learn from her mistakes.

This was not the first or second time we had an incident with scissors, but it was about the eighth time she had cut her hair or someone else's—yes, she has even cut someone else's hair, not to mention the amount of times she has cut her clothing. I made it very clear that Ashley was not to have scissors at school without supervision at any time. I was on my way to pick up Grant, so I decided to march down to Ashley's classroom and check out the damage. I set my three-year-old and my four-year-old on the bright-colored stripe that lined the hallway to Ashley's class. I pulled Ashley out of class and sat her right beside the other two. I had six beautiful, big eyes of various colors staring right at me, wondering what on earth was about to happen. I said, "So Ash, have you had a good day?"

"Yep."

"Oh, good. Nothing has happened at school today?"

"Nope."

"You haven't done anything at school to get in trouble today?"

"Nope, I have been very good." Remember now that I am staring at her with these blond spikes framing her sweet, round, fair face. They may have been about a quarter of an inch, and they went all the way across her forehead.

"You didn't cut your hair?"

"No, Mommy. I promise!"

My mommy voice had been turned on by now, and I was probably on about a six on the volume scale of one to ten. I decided to be very specific. "Ashley, did you take scissors and cut your hair today in class right above your eyes?"

"Nope, sure didn't!"

I then said, "Ashley, I am looking at you right now." I felt four other eyes turn from me toward her from my little babies who were sitting so still and quiet, eagerly awaiting the truth as I was. "I can see you have cut your bangs. Your hair is sticking straight up all the way around your face, and you are going to sit here, look me in the eyes, and tell me you didn't do it?"

"Mommy, I promise I did not cut my hair," I heard between bellowing wells of tears.

I gave up trying to get the truth at this point. It simply

was not going to happen. She still says she didn't cut her hair. Did I mention there were witnesses?

We try very hard to understand and determine the difference between Ashley being confused—such as the temperature, the car wrecks and the death of Steve Irwin—and actually lying. It is amazing to me how clever she can be and how much she puts into getting the lie exactly how it needs to be to try to cover all of her bases. However, she refuses to put any effort into telling the truth. She will look at you with a blank stare for an hour without any sound rather than tell the truth. Our fear is that strangers will not be able to determine the difference.

Ashley's first picture with bangs ... after several months of growth

STEALING

I just know one day I am going to walk out of Target, probably buying another comforter, the alarm is going to go off, and Ashley will have put something that she *really wanted* in her pocket. The nice policeman will ask me how I want to handle it. *Hmm, should I have him haul her in and pray that she will finally learn by her mistakes, or do I play the "special needs" card and say she had no idea what she was doing? Will he even believe me? Will he take me in instead? Will the state take away my children because they think I am teaching my children to steal? Do I adjust my routine and never take her shopping again to avoid any danger of having her there with me? Why can't it just be easy?*

We tried some of the same disciplining tactics for stealing as we have for lying, but the truth is that there is not any discipline that seems to work on Ashley. She could care less about anything except for her best friend, Faith, who by the way, she has stolen from, and Faith was the other person whose hair Ashley cut!

Stealing is another common thread between most children with fetal alcohol syndrome. Why? I don't know. I think it is something they have little to no control over, and it is possible they are trying to fill a void similar to the reason they drink, do drugs, and become sexually promiscuous.

I can remember the first time I found something in her drawer that I knew was not hers. It was some chocolate candy. At first she swore to me she did not know how it got there. Finally she told me Aunt Kristin gave it to her. I immediately called Kristin just to see if that was the truth. We did not have a reason to diagnose Ashley or even have a cause for concern as far as lying goes. I just wanted to have all my ducks in a row before I sat down with her and tried to teach her the importance of truth. As it turned out, she did get the candy from Kristin's house, but Kristin knew nothing about it. We then sat down and had the "truth talk," taking every opportunity I could to parent the way I knew God wanted me to.

I did not think much about it until I started finding other items in her drawers, nightstand, and under her bed. These are still her favorite places—actually the only places—she hides things. You would think she would learn to hide them in new places, but again, that never crosses her mind. For that, I am thankful. At least I don't have to look too far when I am checking up on her.

The stealing has gotten worse; now it has happened at school. She sees something she really wants, and she just takes it. She even stole from her teacher. Thank goodness she has had the same teacher for two years. The teacher really understood Ashley and knew how to handle her. I can't help but wonder what her classmates and their parents thought.

MANIPULATION

Ashley has mastered the art of manipulation, which is another very common trait with FAS. This trait interests me quite a bit. It amazes me that some aspects of life are so incredibly difficult for Ashley to understand yet it takes a very smart person to manipulate people. Ashley is in fact very smart in the sense of having what some people call "street smarts."

She knows she can't get away with it at home because David and I know what she is doing. School, however, is a different story. She usually takes advantage of substitute teachers. I can count on getting a call from the school on any given day that the regular classroom teacher is gone.

Ashley will either have a potty accident or go to the bathroom and put water on her pants to pretend she had an accident. I asked her if it bothered her that other nine and ten-year-olds see her have accidents, and she said, "No, why would that bother me?" She can actually make herself throw up or she will go to the bathroom and say she threw up. She also manipulates people by pretending to be sick just to try to get out of class for a while.

She manipulates family and friends as well that are not around her very much. She will put on a beautiful smile and love on someone to get the affection that she craves. She will make up stories to make them feel sorry for her. For example, she knows how to wrap her grandparents around her little finger. She will tell them the most pitiful story about how she is treated at school or at home, and they will feel so sorry for her and actually get mad at us for something we have done. But the truth is, it never happened.

There have been several times when she has had to apologize to Brooke. When she goes to give Brooke a sincere hug, she will look at me with the scariest look that I interpret as an attempt to threaten me for making her apologize. I never imagined I would have a child that could be so manipulative that I would be scared of her.

ANGER

Controlling her anger is sometimes impossible for Ashley and something she has struggled with since we have known her. I can remember as new parents, we were so inexperienced. One night, when Ashley was around twenty-three months old, she started crying. Of course, we tried to comfort her. We rocked, we sang, we prayed, but to no avail. The harder we tried, the more infuriated she became. She was screaming uncontrollably.

I can remember laying her on the floor at the foot of the rocking chair and looking up at David with huge tears pouring down my face, thinking I was failing as a parent. Ashley was spinning in circles, throwing a huge fit. We did not have a clue what to do. We tried for hours to settle her down.

Finally, we knew we needed sleep, and we were convinced that we had done all we could do. So we moved the port-a-crib into the laundry room. We had a huge laundry room, and it was on the other end of the house rather than on the other side of our bedroom wall like her nursery was located. We knew she would be safe. We knew the sound would be muffled somewhat.

She screamed all night long. After literally being up all night, I walked into the laundry room early the next morning. Ashley just looked at me and smiled like nothing had ever happened. Evidence of the night before, however, was on her arms. She had bitten herself all the way up both arms. I was devastated. We were so scared to tell anybody what had happened. We thought we had tortured her somehow by putting her in the laundry room. That was just the beginning.

Ashley still throws tantrums like that over the least little thing. She can control it somewhat better thanks to therapy and medication. She finally quit biting herself that badly, but in an all-out rage, she can still do major damage to herself and to others. She chokes herself, pinches herself, kicks, hits, and continues to pull chunks of her own hair out. I try to keep her brother and sister at a safe distance so she does not harm them during one of her fits of frustration. There are times, however, when they will be playing so sweetly and then I hear a wrenching scream only to find out Ashley has choked, squeezed, or hit one of them.

One time, I scolded her for writing on the armoire in her room. She went completely ballistic. She started kicking, screaming, and throwing furniture. I tried to sit down on top of her to control her, but she put her foot against my chest and kicked me approximately six feet across the room. I finally had to shut the door and keep her in there until the mood passed. I noticed the yelling had ceased, so I went into her room and talked to her for a minute. I could tell she was remorseful. We hugged and told each other we were sorry and we loved each other.

I asked her if she would like to join us in the kitchen, and she said sure. She walked from her bedroom to the kitchen and met up with Brooke, who was maybe four. Brooke said hi to her and asked her if she was feeling better, then Ashley slapped her across the face. The moment she did it, she turned around and looked at me with a heartbreaking, regretful gaze. I don't think she had any idea why it happened. She went back to her room for the rest of the evening.

Things like this are so difficult to explain to Brooke, and I fear Ashley will teach Brooke and Grant these behaviors. I have to continue to pray that they will choose positive behavior and know the difference between what is right and wrong, unlike their big sister. Anger goes along with frustration, and jealousy sometimes plays a crucial role just as in any sibling relationship; however, Ashley does not understand some of the normal sibling rivalries. Ashley is not allowed to bathe with Brooke anymore because we caught her holding Brooke under the water. We have also caught her stepping on Grant's neck, holding a pillow over Brooke's head, and pushing them down the stairs.

One psychiatrist described Ashley as "unintentionally dangerous." Because of this, I try to constantly keep Ashley separated from Brooke and Grant. I describe it as living in a glass house with sharp edges. I have to be able to see everyone at all times and protect everyone at all times from injury. With my personality, I also try to keep all the glass spotless at the same time. It is a constant stressor that causes me the most worry. I have tried to talk to friends and family about my fears of not being able to protect any of them from Ashley, including protecting Ashley from herself. No one seems to understand, and some tell me it is just sibling rivalry.

The difference is that Ashley does not know when to stop. She doesn't recognize that those horrible screams of terror are exactly that. The kids are in complete terror. Not only does she not recognize the signs to stop, but she does not learn from her mistakes. Of course, she is remorseful sometimes because she has caused someone pain, but other times, she even seems to lack emotion where that is concerned. She has also hurt several little kids at school. I anticipate someone will eventually knock her socks off when she goes after him or her.

We have tried to teach her coping mechanisms such as breathing techniques and appropriate items to squeeze, but she continues to keep hurting herself and anything that might get in her way. Giving her an object to squeeze is an issue in itself, because she ends up using it inappropriately by chewing on it. Then I am concerned with the whole choking thing again. There really is not a win/win solution.

When I stop to think about how frustrated, even angry,

she is all the time because her life is so out of her control, I can actually understand. I am just the opposite. I am a complete control freak, and when things happen that are out of my control, I too have a difficult time handling it. I can't imagine everything in my life being that way. Maybe that is why Ashley and I butt heads so often. No matter what I do, it is difficult to get a grip on how to raise her. I can't even understand why she does the things she does much less how to deal with her when she does it.

DISCIPLINE

We have tried every type of parenting skill we know of in relation to discipline. We have taken away privileges, but that doesn't seem to work because she doesn't really have anything she truly enjoys. We have taken away toys, and again, that doesn't work because she doesn't actually get the concept of toys. I remember how much fun she used to have with toys when we first got her. I wish I understood when and where all of that changed.

Any type of punishment only sends her into an uncontrollable tirade, causing her to stop breathing and start hyperventilating. Sending her to her room for some quiet time seems to work the best, but unfortunately, it does not work every time. She yells, screams, throws things, pulls her hair, pinches herself, and claws the walls for a while. It's not necessarily "quiet" time. I don't know that sending her to her room actually teaches her a lesson, but it allows her time to calm down, and, honestly, allows time for me to refocus as well.

I don't know if it is a good thing to allow her so much time to herself, because she turns to her imaginary friends. I hear her talking to them the entire time she is in her room. They are her rock, so to speak. They keep her grounded and out of trouble. She needs them, and I need for her to have them right now. I make a point to keep a baby monitor close to her room to listen to her conversations with Iyla, Tawnee, and Loloa. It helps me to know what she is thinking. Otherwise, she does not openly discuss her thoughts.

SCHOOL

School has never been Ashley's favorite thing not that her first black eye had anything to do with it. She used to love it, but the more difficult school has become and the more independence that is required, the more she dislikes it. We did make one of the best decisions we have made by having her repeat kindergarten. Although she was very upset to have to stay behind when her other classmates discussed going to first grade, she met her best friend, Faith, during her second year in kindergarten.

Faith is a twin and was born prematurely; therefore, she has some vision issues and wears glasses like Ashley, which gives them a unique similarity. I know with all my heart that Faith is another gift from God. They are separated now because of school districts, but they still remain best friends. Faith is the only *real* friend Ashley has. They understand each other, and, as the saying goes, they complete each other.

Ashley recently had one of her rough days, which can be identified "the moment her feet hit the ground," as we say. It was one of those mornings that it was tough to get her out of bed. She finally got up, sat down on the potty, and just started crying. It did not matter what we said to her or how we talked to her, she was going to roll that head straight back, open her mouth up as wide as it would possibly go, and begin to wail. If we asked her what was wrong, she would just cry uncontrollably and say, "I don't know." I walked her into the classroom so I could let the teacher in on what kind of morning we had, and I informed the nurse as well. Within minutes, I saw Ashley coming down the hall still crying.

Fully prepared, I got a call about an hour later to come get her from school. I decided to take her to the doctor to run some tests to make sure everything was okay with her hormones. Several of the doctors and nurses attempted to talk to Ashley that day, and no one could get her to crack a smile. She kept her arms crossed tightly and her bottom lip out, and she was not going to change her tune.

All of a sudden, I heard a voice outside the door that I recognized. I pulled open the door and in the middle of the afternoon on a school day. There stood Faith in the hallway of the doctor's office, right outside of Ashley's door. She was there for a visit herself, but I know God sent her to be with Ashley.

Ashley jumped up off the table and ran to Faith. They hugged each other with their little blond, blue-eyed heads on each other's shoulders with glasses resting on each side. They started jumping up and down. Ashley's tears turned into happy tears as she told Faith how much she missed her. They began talking this "twin speak" that no one could understand but them.

Faith held Ashley's hand during the blood work, and Ashley became this fun-loving, happy child again. The entire doctor's office was in tears and full of emotional astonishment. After seeing Faith for those few minutes, Ashley wanted to go back to school. She was great the rest of the day.

I know that not all schools are equipped to handle children when they behave like Ashley. We are so fortunate to have found a school that is willing to go far beyond the call of duty to ensure that Ashley succeeds daily. Each person involved with Ashley at school truly loves her and has a deep desire to understand her. It is so important to find a safe and comforting school environment for any child with special needs. School can be overwhelming for them, and they need to know it's okay to be themselves, but they also need to learn about respect.

When Ashley has a meltdown or a defiant day at school where she crosses her arms and refuses to participate and refuses to obey the teacher, they give her the choice of going to the the special education classroom where the heaven-sent teacher, Mrs. Neill is located. In that room Mrs. Neill can calmly get her back to a functioning or somewhat tolerable behavior. She refers to Mrs. Neill as the lady she gets to spend time with when she has a "bad day."

I know I can go to the school at any time to check on Ashley and they know they can contact me at any time to discuss her behavior. We bounce ideas off of each other and we try to incorporate the same discipline techniques at home and school for consistency. We meet at least once a year to have an ARD. The acronym stands for Admission, Review, and Dismissal. The ARD is actually a process to determine eligibility and resources for children with special needs. The ARD process takes place in the form of a meeting. During Ashley's ARD, her entire team gets together to discuss what is best for Ashley. We discuss her progress, her delays, any testing that has taken place, and then we put together a plan for the next year.

These meetings are very important, and as a parent with a child with special needs, the input the parent gives is the most important part of the meeting. I used to worry that I might step on toes if I suggested something different or did not agree with what they wanted to do. I quickly realized that the teachers and administrators in our particular school welcomed the input from the parents. They eagerly look forward to thinking outside of the box to do whatever is best for the child.

Ashley receives several therapies at school and gets assistance throughout the day to get her work completed. She still needs quite a bit of individualized help. She does not understand all of her work, and it takes her a long time to get half of her work finished which is a goal. Her IQ is in the low 80's. Half of the American population has an IQ between 90 and 110 with the average score being 100. Anything below 90 falls into the special needs category and anything above 110 falls into the gifted category.

Faith and Ashley, the best of friends

SLEEPING

Ashley is several years behind in many ways. She still needs a nap and does extremely well when she does have the opportunity to get additional sleep. They don't nap anymore in her class, of course, which is really difficult. We make every effort to get her to sleep by 7:30 and not a minute later. She doesn't sleep well unless she is in her own bed, and even at that, she has to take some medicine that helps to reduce anxiety and calm her nerves to get her to sleep.

Ashley is so full of anxiety that any type of change—whether it is going to bed at a different time, going to bed in a different place, a change in the weather, or even a change of sheets—her little body and mind just can't grasp the newness, and therefore, sleep is out of the question. She will inquire to see if we will still be there when she wakes up and if it will be light or dark outside. I can't understand why she asks these questions. We are always there when she wakes up. I often wonder if she can actually remember a time before we got her of waking up all alone in a dark, cold, empty place. Who knows? If it happened, was she hungry? Did that create the fears?

She tends to hear noises and wonders what is going on and can't get to sleep most of the time. We have found that sleeping with a loud fan or other noisemaker helps tremendously.

She wakes up very early. We have to give her strict rules on what she can do when she wakes up. She has to make sure the clock says at least 7:00 a.m. on weekends before she can turn on the television. Even then, she has to stay in her bed. One weekday morning I heard something on the monitor at 3:00 a.m., and she was in the bathtub getting ready for school.

If we are on vacation or spending the night with friends or family, we can always guarantee she will not sleep at all, which makes for a rough trip. She will, however, sleep all the way home in the security of her own vehicle knowing we are right there. Because of her lack of sleep on trips she behaves very badly which makes it almost impossible to travel with her but there are very few people we can leave her with.

APPEARANCE

Everyone knew Ashley was going to have some developmental delays when she was first taken into custody by the state, but no one, especially the birthmother, especially not us, was prepared for what the future would reveal.

Even though the genetic testing confirmed that Ashley did not have Down's syndrome, she does carry a lot of the physical and mental characteristics. Her body, for instance, has a protruding tummy due to poor posture from weak abdominals. She has short fingers on pudgy but cute hands. These attributes cause the simplest of tasks, such as holding a pencil or a utensil, very difficult for her. The task of wiping herself, bathing herself, combing her hair, and buttoning her own clothes continues to be very difficult and frustrating for her.

Her feet are wider and shorter than normal, causing difficulties with her balance. Tennis shoes seem to be the best solution in most cases, not only for her coordination, but they are simply more comfortable. Tennis shoes, however, bring to the table an entirely new problem: tying them. This is a task that seems to be completely unattainable, not to mention getting them on the right feet in order to get to the next step. For us, the solution that works best is tennis shoes with Velcro closures rather than strings. She has very awkward, uncontrolled movements, sometimes with delays in her fine and gross motor skills.

Ironically, she also has many characteristics of autism as well regarding sensory issues, social issues and "stemming" or constantly moving back and forth or flapping her hands. Children with FAS crave social interaction but do not know how to handle themselves in a social situations where as children with autism realize they do not know how to handle social situations so therefore most of them do not crave the interaction.

I remember reading one time that the most challenging aspect of FAS is the fact that a lot of times their appearance seems normal. Please make note that people do not have to have any physical identifying features to have FAS. Even though Ashley has some of the characteristics of Down's syndrome or autism, she looks and appears normal to most people, which makes it very difficult to explain to people that she isn't "normal." I have heard so many people tell me they just don't see what I see in Ashley. Once they are around her numerous times, they begin to understand, but it does take a while.

SUPPORT

There is no cure or quick fix for fetal alcohol syndrome. Ashley will more than likely need therapy or special assistance for the rest of her life. We will always give her as much as she needs, if not more than she needs. We will never give up. Asking friends, educators, physicians, and other therapists about everything they are doing and everything that is available helps us to stay in the know of everything from which Ashley might benefit.

With all the behaviors Ashley displays and all the time and energy it takes to raise her, there are times when

David and I desperately need a break. This is very difficult because it is hard to find a sitter who understands Ashley. It is very challenging to keep up with Ashley and Grant if a relationship has not been developed. Therefore, David and I do not get much time to ourselves. As wonderful as our parents may be, they are not equipped to take care of the kids for more than a couple of hours at a time, because they do not live in the same town to truly understand what our daily lives entail.

I would love to open a home for children and families with special needs that is fully staffed with appropriately educated, loving adults who could take care of the kids for a short time so parents could feel comfortable going to the grocery store, going out to dinner, or even going away for the weekend.

MEDICATIONS

When Ashley was first diagnosed, we were against medicating her. Not long afterward, we decided that we would be willing to try anything to help her adjust better in school. Once she started school, she changed drastically in just a couple of weeks, and her sweet, soft-spoken self, her beautiful smiles, and her self-confidence rapidly diminished. She was forced into a structured environment that caused a lot of stress for her. We finally decided to try something that would help a little with depression and help her focus. We adjusted strengths and then ultimately switched medications.

I think we have tried everything they have on the market right now that is appropriate for Ashley's diagnosis and age. We finally pulled her off of everything for a while because she was either gaining tons of weight or she was a walking zombie, but her behavior was still the same. That did not last long because we realized not medicating Ashley was far worse on her self-esteem than medicating her.

We also tried medicines for ADD/ADHD, which Ashley definitely has, but it was a horrible experience for all of us. The behavior specialist put her on the medication, and it was like "pouring fuel on a fire," according to our pediatrician. We have since learned that it is never a good idea to treat FAS children with ADD/ADHD medications. The medication that seems to work best for Ashley is an anti-psychotic medication called Seroquel. It helps her sleep, which helps her to focus. Sleep also helps her with her moods. Please keep in mind that I am no expert. My intent is just to share our personal experience and pray that it helps at least one family.

THERAPY

Therapy is a must with children with FAS, but for us it has also been very frustrating. I am a firm believer in the benefits of early intervention. That is why I feel it is so important to seek medical expertise at the first sign of concerns with any child.

Since we first met Ashley, she has had some form of therapy. She received help from Early Childhood Intervention as soon as the state found her due to her developmental delays at the time. I was an early childhood specialist at one time, so I thought I could help her more than anyone and I took over that responsibility as soon as she came to live with us. I quickly realized she needed help from other therapeutic disciplines, so I found a speech therapist, physical therapist, and occupational therapist for her. The occupational therapist referred her to a sensory integration therapist. Once we finally moved to

Lubbock, she started feeding therapy, hippotherapy, and vision therapy.

As much therapy as she has received, I have to ask myself how much of it is really helping. I have seen some changes but not huge leaps and bounds. I would never pull her out of anything I knew she needed. My concern is if she will need these therapies for the rest of her life, will she be able to help herself get to therapy if I am not there to push her? Will she be able to pay for them?

I also ask myself if there is anything out there that would benefit her more that I am not giving her. Although it is not necessarily a "therapy" I have to say that the one thing that helps her the most is anything church related and that is something I will gladly provide. Being actively involved with God and in our church lifts her spirits, gives her confidence and exposes her to other children that also have a deep desire to strengthen their souls.

THE WALK FROM WITHIN

So, my dear brothers and sisters, be strong and steady, always enthusiastic about the Lord's work, for you know that nothing you do for the Lord is ever useless.

1 Corinthians 15:58

I began journaling some daily experiences our family goes through while raising a child with fetal alcohol syndrome. It became a form of therapy for me. I started seeing a difference in the way I handled Ashley and developed a sense of understanding for her that I had not experienced before. I am only going to share a couple of days just to give you an example of our daily walk. These stories do not include anything that my other two little angels are doing in the mix of all the chaos.

We finally had a good … somewhat good day with Ashley. She did not try to hurt anyone, she did not cry one time, and she did not get in trouble at school.

Now that's success! I had the slightest bundle of energy, so I decided it was going to be the day to start journaling. Well, I should have done it while the mood in the house was still good.

I woke up this morning actually encouraged to see her. She sets her alarm at 6:45 so that she can get in the bath and soak for a few minutes before her day starts. This usually helps us get through the first hour of the day just a little easier. I wish I could figure out a way to make the other twenty-three hours easier. Sometimes we get off to a rough start when she turns her clock off early and we find her in the tub at three or five in the morning. She swears her alarm went off. I guess she doesn't think we are smart enough to figure that out. Or maybe she actually thinks her alarm did go off.

Ashley does not sleep very well. The first fifteen minutes went pretty good. Then it became time to bathe her. She will be nine in about three weeks, and she still cannot bathe herself. Thirty minutes later I was still yelling, "Hurry, Ash," as I was getting breakfast ready. She was slowly trying to dress herself. Even after six years of attempting to teach her to dress herself, I am convinced that she will eventually get it. She still puts her panties on inside out, sideways, backwards; it really does not matter to her. The same goes with the rest of her clothes. I don't know if she doesn't care that things are on incorrectly or if she just does not know. I finally got her out the door and on her way to school, and as hard as I tried to make the morning a good one, I noticed she had toothpaste all over the front of her shirt as I finally gave up the thought of her trying to zip her own jacket. I pray every day for God to control my tongue, but after over an hour getting one child ready, my tongue starts swinging out these hurtful words. At that point, I can't control what comes out of my mouth, and I am consumed with guilt immediately afterward. My mind is trying to figure out how she just can't care how she looks or what people think. I just can't grasp the fact that those thoughts are impossible for her to understand.

Ashley devoured her breakfast in a matter of seconds this morning. This is such a poor habit of hers and one that we cannot get a grip on. There are times when she doesn't even chew her food. I was not able to catch her this morning. I asked her to go wash her hands and brush her teeth to go to school. As anticipated, I walked in her bathroom and she was messing around. She was holding the toothpaste cap, filling it up with water, and pouring it on the counter. I looked down, and there was spit up all over the counter. I knew exactly what it was as Ashley has done this since the first day we met her.

She eats and drinks so quickly that she spits up almost like a baby with reflux. We have taken her in for testing and tried various medicines, but nothing has worked. I decided to ask her what she was doing, and of course, she said, "nothing." Then I asked her what was on the counter. She started with the standard answer of nothing and then decided it would be better to say it was already there.

Being the wise and experienced mother that I am, I pointed out that I knew it was spit-up and I knew she was trying to wash it away with her toothpaste cup. I decided to not point out the fact that she was only centimeters from the actual sink and question why she could not have just spit-up in there. After I gave my huge, all-knowing speech, she looked at me with those big, blue eyes that I prayed so long for and said, "I never got the toothpaste." Remember, she has the toothpaste in one hand and the cap in the other. I knew her teacher was going to feel the wrath the remainder of her day.

I left to work out of town after I dropped the kids off. Just as I thought, I got an email from Ashley's teacher. Ashley had decided she did not want to do her work and was asked to move her clip to a different color, which is a behavior discipline method. Ashley refused to move her clip like the teacher asked. Her arms were crossed, and she had decided to spit up on her desk as a full-fledged attempt to get out of the classroom. Thank goodness her teacher knows her well because she did not allow Ashley to leave the classroom like she wanted. Instead, she made her clean up her desk and reminded her that she was there to learn.

We celebrated Ashley's ninth birthday this weekend. It was more evident than ever that Ashley is so different than the other children her age. She is still very immature and does not get the social aspects of life that come so naturally to others. Her sleeping habits are getting worse. She struggles every night because she says she hears people talking and moving around in her room. She even says she feels people touching her on the back. She is extremely paranoid and startles easily.

Ashley started a new medicine last night to help her sleep. She was in a great mood this morning and very talkative. I am eager to hear how her day at school went. Ashley got home late today after going to a ballgame with our sitter.

The day went great. Let's hope it was because of all the wonderful sleep.

When I picked her up from school today, her sleeves were dirty from her wrist to her armpits. How is that possible? How could someone get that dirty? Usually, when I pick her up from school, she still has food all over her face from lunch. That means she has had food on her face for approximately four hours. Does she notice? No. Does she care? No. Should I be upset, or would it be better if no one cared or noticed if we had food on our face? Most of my friends have daughters Ashley's age. They care about their appearance. Not Ashley. She could not care less. Her pants will be unzipped, hanging down past her rear, her hair will be all sticky and in her face, her clothes will be ruined for the day, and food will still be on her face, and she does not even realize she looks out of place.

Tomorrow is Saturday, so I'll have her all day. I should start praying now! We have sold our house, and we are looking for a new one. I'll start packing this weekend as well. Change is not good for Ash. She completely freaks out. I used to send her to a daycare after school so that I could have a little more time with the little ones and a little less time to have to deal with all the "stuff" Ashley dishes out at me. It actually became too much trouble for the daycare. Most people do not understand that you have to watch Ashley like she is a toddler. She is constantly into everything and constantly making poor choices. It almost takes one person watching her nonstop. Her kindergarten teacher was worried about telling us at the end of the year meeting that she had to watch Ashley more than she watched another child in her classroom the year before who had Down's syndrome. Now I don't really get a break from her except for regular school hours. I feel bad that I hate to send the other two to school. I want to be with them all the time. I send them because I know they need it, not because I know I need it.

My devotional today was from 1 John 2:28. "And now, dear children, continue in fellowship with Christ so that when he returns, you will be full of courage and not shrink back from him in shame" (NIV).

Just more reassurance that I need to get my act together, get back in church, and be more accepting of Ashley!

Ashley has been really good all day again today. I was a little worried this morning. I usually say I can tell the minute her feet hit the ground if it is going to be a good day or a bad day. We were all sitting at the bar this morning eating breakfast. I asked Ashley to let the dog outside. She went to the door, let the dog out, and then started circling the table, the living room, and the bar area looking around. She finally found her plate again and sat down to finish her breakfast. I never said anything, but I thought to myself, *Wow! I can't believe she got lost that quickly.*

I was walking behind the rest of the family today as we were trying to get through the airport. Ashley was waving her hands in circles with her head turned to the side and shoulders turned toward the ground while she was in deep conversation with one or more of her imaginary friends. She was bumping into people and walls because, number one, she wasn't looking, and, number two, she was literally walking uncontrollably from one side of the hallway to the other.

Okay, Ashley completely floored me today. We were talking about this book, and I showed her another book that was written by a little girl with FAS. She said, "That's cool, but we can't copy it; that would be boring. That's called plagiarism." Um. Where in the heck did that come from? Half the time—okay, 75 percent of the time—she can't tell her right from her left, but all the sudden she not only knows the word plagiarism but understands it!

DETERMINATION

All along I have tried my best to let wisdom guide my thoughts and actions. I said to myself, "I am determined to be wise." But it didn't really work. Wisdom is always distant and very difficult to find.

Ecclesiastes 7:23–24

When Ashley was about five years old, she brought me a little piece of red plastic. It was obvious to me that it had broken away from a very well-loved toy. She thought it was one of the most beautiful things she had ever seen. She said in the sweetest, most genuine voice, "Oh Mommy, don't you love it? Isn't it beautiful?" She then asked if I knew where its parent's were. I began to tell her that yes, I thought it was very pretty and it looked very special but that it was a piece of plastic and it did not have parents. She looked up at me almost breathless and said, "Oh no; well, we could always adopt it."

As tears welled up in my eyes, I tried to sort out her tattered understanding on life. She obviously understood that we adopted her to love her and take care of her because her biological parents could not, but yet she could not determine the difference between human beings and pieces of plastic. I can't imagine going through life so confused yet so wise in so many ways.

Writing this book has been much of the same experience for me. I have expressed confusion and gained wisdom, as well as regained my sanity. Just the other day, when Ashley was having a meltdown, David was getting frustrated, and I simply said, "David, that is not how she understands it. She can't help it." He never said anything else until we got in bed later that night. He told me he wanted to compliment me on something. He noticed a difference in me with the way I handled Ashley. I told him thank you, and I realized I had noticed a huge difference in myself as well.

This book started as a journaling process to vent when I was frustrated with her and at a loss for how to handle her behavior. At the same time, I began praying for wisdom for each and every decision we made, whether it was regarding financial issues, raising our children, or getting more actively involved in a new church home. Most importantly, I prayed for a better relationship with Ashley, more understanding toward her, and a softer heart for her. Within days, I could feel the difference. Not only have all my prayers been answered, but we now have a church home to call our very own, and she has asked Jesus to live in her heart.

I have discovered new ways to motivate her to get things done and to love life. I have developed a relationship with her again. We hold hands. I know that sounds small, but it is really big. I think for a while I was actually resentful toward her. I was not dumb enough to believe all of our hardships and struggles were her fault, but I was dumb enough to treat her as if I did blame her.

I know now that I cannot change her, but as I learned in college, I can change myself with the help of God. I just need the courage to change and the wisdom to know when change is needed. I have been so blessed. I have beautiful, wonderful, healthy children, and God selected each one of them for me and me for them. He definitely had a plan, and he selected me to follow through with that plan. I am determined to get this book out for Ashley and all the other children, as well as their families who are challenged with this preventable disorder. I am determined to devote my life to my family again rather than hiding behind the diagnosis, my work, or my disappointment in how I have handled everything. So many people make the comment about how strong I am and how well I handle everything. I must put on a pretty good exterior appearance because on the inside I feel like I have been running a never-ending marathon.

I know I am not perfect, but I do not want to have any more regrets or shame. It is my job to get the word out on the dangers of drinking alcohol during pregnancy. I even hope I can get legislation to pass to make it illegal for a pregnant woman to drink. I know without a doubt that this book will help at least one person, and maybe it will reach another person that can use the information to help millions.

I want to thank you for devoting your time to read this book. I hope you have grown to know Ashley and love her. I also pray that you will share this book with anyone and everyone you know that is pregnant, thinking about becoming pregnant, drank during pregnancy, or counsels women. I pray that together, it can become a world-wide mission to stop the abuse done to these innocent babies before they even enter this world that can be cruel even without marks against them. Help me stop some of the loss of sanity that is unwillingly forfeited by these precious angels who God created.

After fourteen years of praying for a blond, blue-eyed angel, I have a new prayer now that I found in a very inspirational book by Stormie Omartian, called *The Power Of A Praying Parent*. I inserted Ashley's name into the prayer.

> "Lord, I pray that [Ashley] be given the gift of joy. Let the spirit of joy rise up in her heart this day and may she know the fullness of joy that is found only in your presence. Help her to understand that true happiness and joy are found only in you. Whenever she is overtaken by negative emotions, surround her with your love. Teach her to say, "This is the day that the Lord has made, we will rejoice and be glad in it" (Psalm 118:2). Deliver her from despair, depression, loneliness, discouragement, anger, or rejection. May these negative attitudes have no place in [Ashley], nor be a lasting part of her life. May she decide in her heart, "My soul shall be joyful in the Lord; it shall rejoice in His salvation" (Psalm 35:9). I know, Lord, that any negative emotions this child feels are lies, contrary to the truth of your Word. Plant your word firmly in her heart and increase her faith daily. Enable her to abide in your love and derive strength from the joy of the Lord this day and forever."

I know that it is difficult for Ashley to control her actions, but I am blessed to know that God has complete control. God knows what the future holds for Ashley, and I pray for understanding daily.

FROM ASHLEY'S HEART

What do you think about Mommy writing a book all about you?

I like it because no one else in my class has a book about them.

What does fetal alcohol syndrome mean?

It means you drink a bad drink when you have a baby in your tummy. It makes the baby break their glasses, break stuff, and say no to the teacher when they growed up.

How does fetal alcohol syndrome make you feel?

Worried sometimes.

About what?

About smoking and doing bad stuff when I grow up.

What is your favorite thing to do?

Besides sing? Play with Faith.

Is there anything you wish you could do?

Drive.

What is the most important thing to you?

Read.

What do you want to be when you grow up?

I really want to be an artist.

How will you become an artist?

By getting good grades on my art and not getting out of the lines.

Is there anything else you want me to write in the book?

I have a little sister and a little brother.